Stagecoach to Birdsville

STAGECOACH TO BIRDSVILLE

HELEN FERBER

Kangaroo Press

Cover Design by Darian Causby
Main photo: Cobb and Co. Coach at Renmark, c. 1890
Courtesy of the State Library of South Australia (B11355)

© **Helen Ferber**

First published in 1995 by Kangaroo Press Pty Ltd
3 Whitehall Road Kenthurst NSW 2156 Australia
P.O. Box 6125 Dural Delivery Centre NSW 2158
Printed by Southwood Press Marrickville

ISBN 0 86417 694 5

Contents

Metric Equivalents

Where imperial measures have been retained, the approximate equivalents are:

1 mile	=	1.61 kilometres
1 pound (lb)	=	454 grams
1 inch	=	25.4 millimetres
1 foot (ft)	=	0.3048 metres

Money

12 pence (d.)	=	1 shilling (s.), also written as 1/–
20 shillings	=	1 pound (£)

When decimal currency was introduced in 1966 two Australian dollars was the equivalent of one pound, but this does not enable us to translate nineteenth-century prices into those of today.

Temperature

$$°C = \frac{°F - 32}{1.8}$$

Acknowledgments

I acknowledge with thanks a grant from the Victorian Ministry of the Arts towards research for this book.

Two people have given me invaluable assistance: my husband, David, who has been my constant helper and encourager, as willing to delve in French and German archives as to trek up the Birdsville Track; and my friend, Isabel Seddon, who made thoughtful comments on successive drafts, in between episodes of eye surgery.

Frances Gage McGinn very generously sent me and gave me permission to use a photograph of Mrs Ward which appeared in her book, *Birdsville.*

I am indebted, too, to staff at the State Library of South Australia for making available to me the photographs of the Cobb and Co. coach, the camels harnessed to a heavy load for the outback, and the flowers on sand dunes on the Birdsville Track; to staff at the Museum of Port Pirie, who copied for me the invaluable *Glimpses of Napperby Since 1840;* and to the Royal Geographical Society of Australasia (South Australian Branch) Inc., for making available to me their notes for participants in their Haddon Corner safari of September 1985.

And last but by no means least, I thank Mrs Ilse Lange, of Celle in Hanover, Germany, who preserved the Hoche papers when the last member of the Hoche family in Germany had died and took the trouble to trace me, a complete stranger, and pass them on to me.

Helen Ferber
1995

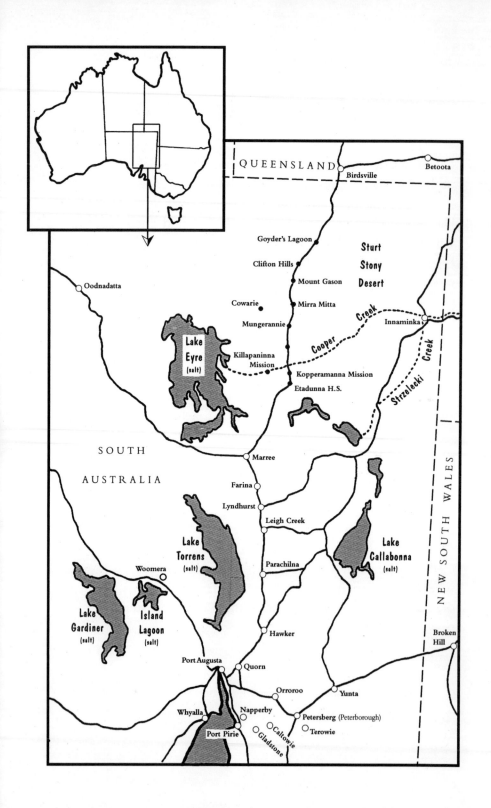

1

'I take up my pen'

'I now take up my pen to inform you that I have given up all thoughts of marrying,' wrote Eleanor Dingley Ferry to her friend Fanny in July 1886. Eleanor was my grandmother and fortunately for me and for her other descendants she was to abandon this rather extreme stand not long afterwards. Fortunately, too, the habit of taking up her pen at frequent intervals stayed with her to the end of her days. And perhaps because of the circumstances in which her days ended most of the letters she wrote were kept by her family and friends and eventually came down to me.

Eleanor, or Nellie as she was called by her family, grew up in what today would be called genteel poverty, a poverty from which marriage offered her and her sisters the only hope of escape. She was born in 1867 in Morphett Vale in South Australia, the seventh out of the fourteen children of John and Emma Ferry (née de la Hant). John had arrived in South Australia from England in 1853, at the age of twenty-one, with his school teacher parents, John Mattinson Ferry and Mary Ferry, three brothers and three sisters. Emma de la Hant, who, although of French ancestry, had grown up in London's East End, arrived a year later with her parents, sister and brother. She and John were married in 1857.

Like his parents, John Ferry was a school teacher, having taught from an early age in his father's boarding school at Edmonton, outside London. He was only eighteen when in 1850 his father's health broke down and he had to take over the running of the school, assisted by his fourteen-year-old sister, Cecilia, while their mother cared for the boarders. When his father was advised to move to a warmer climate, it was John who suggested going to South Australia rather than the south of France. A family friend who had settled in Adelaide not long before had been sending glowing accounts of life in the new colony.

In South Australia John taught in a succession of small country schools, none of which, even with a small state stipend to supplement the fees, afforded him enough to provide more than the bare necessities for his ever-growing family. Each pupil attending school paid ninepence or one shilling a week, though for poor children only sixpence was paid by the state. But these fees were paid only when the children actually attended, and since children, particularly boys, were frequently kept home from school when required for work on the farm or in the house, a schoolmaster's income fluctuated. Small quarterly stipends, ranging from £40 to £80 per annum, were paid by the Board of Education to supplement fees, the amount reflecting the attainments of the teachers, the results of their teaching, the number of their scholars and the number of people living within reach of their respective schools.[1] Since John Ferry taught in small new schools in fledgling townships, it is hardly surprising that his income was small.

Emma Ferry was obliged to help her husband in the schoolroom. A childhood illness had left John with impaired hearing, so at all his schools it was she who took the reading classes. For this she was not paid. Had John not been an excellent teacher, it seems unlikely that with such a handicap he could have made a career as a teacher, though an early Board of Education report indicates there were difficulties in finding good teachers of reading. 'There are so few good readers among teachers, any more than among other classes of persons, that the advantage of example is too often wanting to the children.'[2] That John was deaf must have been known to the Board of

Education, for an inspector's report at his last school, at Napperby, noted: 'The children are inclined to take advantage of the teacher's defective hearing.'[3] But the Board of Education not only retained John: it also on at least two occasions moved him to a bigger school with higher attendances, in recognition of his need to provide for a large family. One factor, perhaps, in the Board's favourable view of him was his excellent handwriting, for parents set particular store by their children's handwriting prowess, one aspect of their education that they felt they could judge. The popularity of a school depended on it.[4]

John Ferry's handwriting

Emma had had no experience of teaching, but as a child in London she had a very strict governess who saw that she gained an excellent command of the English language. In addition to taking the reading classes she was responsible for teaching needlework and for this the Board paid her a small allowance. At some of their schools she and John also offered an evening class, as a means of increasing their income, for it was better paid than day school: provided a class was held on two evenings a week for more than three months it attracted a weekly Board of Education payment of two shillings a head, in addition to the one shilling a week the pupils themselves paid. That it was money hard-earned is clear from a letter John wrote to his eldest son from his second last school, at Terowie near Port Pirie, in which he mentioned 'the probability of a good evening school after ploughing is finished'. At every post he and Emma tried to grow as much as possible of the family's food.

Accommodation, too, was a problem and added to the family's financial difficulties: they usually arrived at a new post to find no more than two rooms in the teacher's house, being obliged at one place to rent at their own expense a second house, with five rooms, next door. At another post the only entrance to the schoolroom was through one of the two rooms in which the family had to live. Sometimes it was 'girls into the spring cart, boys under the wagon' until additions could be made to the house, usually by John and his sons and often at John's own expense. The Board of Education's annual reports indicate that it was by no means unusual for country teachers to have to add to, or provide, their own accommodation, sometimes even the schoolroom.

Like many of their schoolmates, the Ferry boys started working for others at age eleven or twelve, one with a country mail route, others on vineyards and farms at seed time and harvest or haymaking. When not bringing extra money into the household one of the older boys would be sent to help his ageing grandfather, who was teaching at Meningie, or to be a companion to his grandmother, left by herself 'from nine o'clock till four, with only a rather savage dog, tied so that it controlled the walk to the kitchen and backdoor', to protect her against a possible Aboriginal attack (which as far as we know never eventuated).

The girls in the family were not sent out to work but helped at home from a very early age. As the arrival of a new baby was almost an annual event, Emma found it necessary to organise a division of labour for the performance of the household tasks. She herself cared for the newborns until they were weaned; she also did some of the cooking, cut out the family's clothes, kept an overall eye on things and, of course, helped in the school. Once the babies were weaned her eldest daughter, also Emma, took over their care, although little more than a child herself. (A grandson in his memoirs referred to her little charges as the 'ex-babies'.) She also did the baking. When the next daughter, Mary Louisa, was old enough she took over the sewing of the clothes, helped by her younger sisters. Keeping sixteen people in clothes, and sewing by hand everything from underwear to trousers and overcoats, was a major undertaking. It was a rather triumphant John who eventually arrived home with a second-hand sewing machine, 'a lockstitch Wheeler and Wilson', though initially he was the only one who could work it and later needed to be on call 'to dissolve trouble'.

As the older girls married, the younger ones took their place on the home front, or were despatched to keep house for older brothers working elsewhere or to help their married sisters with young children. This was to be Nellie's lot, and she did not relish the role. 'Baby is a very cross little thing,' she wrote of a little niece whom she was helping to care for at Quorn, a new and raw little town beyond Port Augusta. She was by now a very lively nineteen, ('rather waggish' was how one of her cousins was to describe her to her children many years later), and though she joined in the local quadrilles, church concerts, waxworks and horse races, she confided in a letter to

Eleanor "Nellie" Ferry

her best friend, Fanny or Fran Siekmann, that small-town life was dreadfully dull. But she made the best of it and took a great interest in any young men around: 'We have a real spry butcher,' she wrote to Fanny, 'his name is Bob Hotchins. He has a beautiful smile and Arthur [her brother-in-law] always goes to the window when I am taking the meat to see him smile at me . . . Sometimes [he] says: "here's a nice piece, Miss Nell, it'll eat splendid"'.

Then, when Nellie was nineteen and living back with her parents at Napperby near Port Pirie, things began to look up. There was boating, driving, walking and a concert in aid of the Church of England. And there was love: in May 1886 she told Fanny, 'I am in love. I am engaged to a Mr Alfred South. Such a real nice man . . . He is tall and very fair. Really, Fan, you would not believe what a difference it makes. I don't seem the same girl at all.'

But love did not last. Two months later it was over: 'I broke off my engagement last Wednesday, and don't mean to get engaged again in a hurry; and, dear Fan, don't you ever listen to a man— they are all alike, more or less.'

One month after writing this letter she was already feeling less strongly about the opposite sex. She reported to Fanny that the parson from Port Augusta had preached in Port Pirie that day, and had come to tea. 'He stands no less than six foot six in his socks, middlen long for a parson, eh, but he is *very* nice!'

And four months after she had given up all thoughts of marrying she was all set to take the plunge again. No, not to the tall parson, but to a young immigrant doctor from Germany, Edward Hoche. And if the decision to marry was as impulsive as her earlier decision not to, at least she had plenty of time to think it over, for her parents showed a proper caution. Dr Hoche had only arrived in Port Pirie four months earlier (in August 1886) and since inquiries in the German community by a German friend yielded only the meagre information that he was 'well spoken of by people who have been in his company', John Ferry accepted an offer by the German Consul in Adelaide to have discreet inquiries made through a friend of his in Hamburg, the doctor's home town.

In February 1887 the report from Hamburg to the Consul was passed on to the family. Dr Hoche, it said, was the son of the director of a college in Hamburg, a school of world renown. He had completed his medical studies in Göttingen and Berlin, served his time in the army as a surgeon, and made one or two voyages in a steamer to New York. 'In short,' the anonymous investigator went on, 'his past life lies open before me, and not one moment in it cannot be accounted for. He has been kept close to his studies, the position of his father warranting such, and he has not idled away his time. But he has always been of a troublesome adventurous mind, and that, not fitting in with the quiet sedate mode of life at home, has made him, when out of control, kick out a little. He has sown his wild oats a little fast, and that, considering the limited means and large family of his father, has made it desirable that he should be set on his own legs and try his own way in the world. If he was to return and follow up his regular career there would not be the slightest objection to it.'

'I shall be glad', the Consul's friend in Hamburg concluded, 'to learn from you about the young lady and her family and hope we shall have as much cause to congratulate ourselves as they have. If she is a sensible young lady she will find no difficulty in leading a life of happiness with him.'

'I hope *we* shall have as much cause to congratulate ourselves . . .' *'We'* are the Germans, Consul Hugo Muecke and his friend in Hamburg, agreeing that a young woman in Australia would be fortunate to marry a doctor from a solid respectable Hamburg family, no matter what he had been up to. If they knew what form the doctor's youthful kicking out had taken they did not tell the Ferrys, nor did they disclose the nature of the wild oats so lightly dismissed. Events which lay in the future must have made the Ferry family wish they had pressed for more information.

After the Consul's letter had been considered, the engagement was approved. The Hoche family were reported to have received the news quietly, since their son had informed them that his position required his being a married man. They thought him rather young for marrying (he was twenty-six) but since his career in this strange and distant country was now altogether different from the family tradition he must go his own way.

Edward Hoche

No letter survives telling us Nellie thought Edward handsome, like the unfortunate Mr South, or that she loved him. Photographs show him rather stern, slightly bald, rimless pince-nez glasses perched on his nose. Nellie was perhaps in some awe of him for she referred to him always in letters to her family as 'the Dr' or 'the old man'. Only when writing to his family in Hamburg did she refer to him as Edward.

Edward's reasons for marrying may have been far from

romantic. In the very first letter he wrote to his family, in September 1886, just six weeks after his arrival in Port Pirie, he told them:

> It is urgently necessary for me to marry as soon as possible. In practices involving women there is a prejudice here against unmarried doctors, and while I now get a midwife to be present if I am examining women or delivering babies, this is not a long-term solution.

He goes on to speculate rather gloomily on his prospects of finding a suitable wife in Port Pirie:

> I am house doctor to the family of the mayor and he already has some serious ideas about some of the local beauties, but from what I have seen here of the girls of the so-called aristocracy one of these would not suit me at all. These girls do not do anything in the house. In the morning they go visiting or what they call shopping. In the afternoon they play lawn tennis. Cooking does not interest them. They are out late in the evening and go to church three or four times on Sunday, which here is an absolutely dead day. If it were in any way possible I would like to have a wife sent out from Germany, but who? The only one that I had considered is [and here the name has been carefully cut out of the letter, probably by later keepers of the family papers in Hamburg]. If you think it feasible, please make discreet inquiries and write to me about it, and I will answer by return mail.

He concluded by asking his family to let him know the total of the debts he had left behind him, saying he hoped to be able to repay half of them shortly.

Perhaps despatching a wife from Germany proved not to be feasible; perhaps in Eleanor Ferry Edward at last found someone willing and able to perform all the wifely duties, including being present at confinements and the examination of women patients. Perhaps he even fell in love with her. She was pretty, lively and, for her time, well-educated. At all events, after a long engagement they were married in March 1888. They continued to live in Port Pirie, where Edward had been in medical practice since his arrival eighteen months earlier. In his first letter home he had assured his family that there was no better place in the world to practice. A second doctor had come to the town a month after his own arrival, but Edward found his rival's medical knowledge deficient and said his rough manner put people off. He himself had had instant success, and after six weeks had ninety-six patients on his books and had been able to buy himself a carriage and horses. He described Port Pirie as 'a so-called town' of 900 inhabitants but said his practice was largely a country one. He wrote that he had not only learnt English on the voyage out but had studied his medical books hard, expecting to have to pass an examination. However, this had turned out to be unnecessary, as the medical authorities in South Australia had given him the authorisation to practise immediately he sent off his German doctor's diploma.

Doctors' fees, he wrote, were higher than in Germany, even in a country practice. Five shillings extra over and above the fees was payable for every mile travelled, which worked out, for a ten-mile trip, at about £3. Laundry was terribly dear: to have a dozen articles of whatever sort washed cost four shillings and all prices were of that order.

If Edward had continued to do as well in Port Pirie as he claimed to be doing in the early months after his arrival (and by 1891 the population there had increased to 4 000), it is curious that he should have moved in October 1892 to Farina, a much smaller town, which had sprung up 403 kilometres to the north of Port Pirie after the railway line was extended there in 1882. There seems to be one obvious explanation: despite his claim in his first letter to Hamburg that the medical authorities had given him the authorisation to practise, he was not registered as a doctor. In fact, the Registrar of the Medical Board of South Australia can find no record that he ever even applied for registration, although that would seem to indicate a gap in the records, since he had been quite prepared to sit for an examination, if need be, to secure the right to practise. Registration was a requirement for anyone to practise medicine in the colony under the *Medical Practitioners Act (Ordinance No 17 of 1844)*, amended by the Acts of 1880 and 1889.[5] The Act of 1880 states: 'No person shall . . . be deemed to be a legally-qualified medical practitioner, unless such person shall have proved to the satisfaction of the . . . Board that he is possessed of one of the qualifications mentioned in the Schedule hereto, and shall have received from the said Board a certificate of his being a legally-qualified medical practitioner. . .' Item 12 of the schedule, the one relevant to holders of foreign medical qualifications, indicates acceptance of 'any qualification which would entitle the holder to practise in all branches of medicine in any foreign state, and also to hold Government medical appointments in such state'.

There seems to be no obvious reason for Edward Hoche not to have secured registration. His being a foreigner should not have counted against him under the Act of 1880, which would have been in force when he arrived, for we have the German Consul's assurance to the Ferry family that Edward would have been entitled to return to Germany and 'follow up his regular career' had he wished to do so. A Medical Board was set up in 1887 for the registration of properly qualified doctors from outside Australia. Even under the 1889 amendment to the Act, which required a minimum of four years' medical studies and an examination at the end, he should have been qualified, having done his four years at Berlin and Göttingen, universities of world standing at the time. His graduation records from their medical schools show his results to have been very good (the only subject he had ever failed was botany).

So his failure to secure registration remains a mystery. What cannot be ruled out is the possibility of quiet discrimination against foreign doctors by the medical establishment in South Australia. W.F. Morrison, author of the *Aldine History of South*

Australia, believed such discrimination existed. He wrote of the
'glaring injustice' of the system under which the Medical Board
dispensed or withheld registration: 'The law of the land does
not bar any person from the practice of medicine', he wrote,
'but it does make a distinction between a registered and an
unregistered physician. The people have said through legislation
who shall be admitted to registration but the [Medical] Board
are the constituted judges as to whether the applicant is qualified
under the law. Only registered physicians are held to be duly
qualified and only such can be appointed to the several hospitals,
associations, insurance societies, etc., so that physicians and
surgeons of first rank in scholarship may be rejected by the above
Board, and, in the eyes of the law, be unqualified, while, in
reality, they may be, and are sometimes, the peers of any one on
the Board.'[6] Morrison claimed that there was wide suspicion
that the members of the Board, in withholding registration, were
not motivated by a desire to protect the public but by a
determination to further their own interests. Since his history
was published in 1890, Morrison would have been writing this
at the very time Edward was trying unsuccessfully to establish
himself in legitimate practice.

If the lack of a registration certificate had made practice in
Port Pirie impossible, in Farina he was apparently able to practise
quite openly, for Nellie refers in a letter to his going with the
police to 'bring in a poor old black laid up with influenza and
bronchitis at a blacks' camp a few miles out of town'. Perhaps
the impossibility of attracting a registered doctor to such a small
place made the authorities willing to overlook his illegal status.

By the time Edward moved to Farina he and Nellie had two
children, Edith or Pussy, aged three, and Richard Francis, or
Frank, my father, aged two, and Nellie was expecting a third
child. She did not join Edward for some months. In a letter to
his family she mentioned that she had had two miscarriages,
one of which had left her seriously ill, and she was being cared
for by members of her family in or near Port Pirie. When she

finally joined Edward in Farina in April 1893 she left Pussy behind in Port Pirie with her eldest sister, Emma Pearce. Pussy was to remain there nine months. A second son was born in Farina in May 1893 and named Leonard.

Nellie did not want for kindness from the local people. She and Edward and little Frank initially lived at the town's one hotel, and a month before Leonard's birth she wrote to her sister Emma:

> The people here are very kind, and look after me splendidly. They bring me tea and bread and butter at 7 o'clock every morning and at four in the afternoon. Last Sunday I was not very well, had a nasty attack of colic and vomiting, and the old man made me stay in bed. Really, if I had been among my own friends I could not have been looked after better. They [the hotel people] took Frank away for a drive and had beef tea and all sorts of stuff made for me that I did not need.

She concluded by saying she would write later to her younger sisters but for now news was 'devilish scarce'.

Despite the kindness of her Farina neighbours, Nellie missed having family around her, especially when Edward was called to country cases. She commented wistfully in another letter to her family that her younger sisters seemed to be having 'lively times' and that she often wished she could pop in on them for a 'good old gas and grin', and asked for photos of her sisters. (She was particularly fond of her three younger sisters, Edith, who at this stage was twenty-one, Mabel nineteen and Florence or Flossie, thirteen.) But she never complained, making light of any mishaps. Thus when a hurricane struck the town she wrote to her sister Emma:

> On Sunday we had the biggest hurricane I ever saw; nearly all the aunties [outdoor toilets] done the 'disappearin' trick', to say nothing of verandahs etc. I saw our auntie make her bow and depart real graceful, then our next door neighbour's and we began to think the house would be the next, but she is a good sticker, thank goodness.

The Farina hotel where the Hoche family lived

Nellie kept her colourful slangy writing for her sisters and her bosom friend Fanny Siekmann. The one surviving letter from her to Edward's family in Hamburg is written in impeccable English. She was usually careful, too, when writing to her own mother. Apologising for her handwriting in one of her letters to her from Farina, she said she was writing with baby Lennie on her knee: 'I can fancy I hear you saying "what a bad letter Nellie writes, not worth the stamp".'

Frank seems to have thrived in Farina and been so active that he hardly had time to miss his sister. Nellie told Emma:

Little Frank's health is improving wonderfully; you would hardly think he was the same puny little Frankie that left Port Pirie three weeks ago. He eats enough for a boy three times his size, and the little beggar is never at home. He is always out somewhere, and has got quite used to camels and donkeys and is not at all frightened of them. In fact, he has been on a camel. He went to a cricket match on Monday with the Dowlings (police people) and was away the whole of the day and had lunch with no less than four different parties. He talks of Mrs Mansfield as Ma, and when I asked him who Ma was, he said its Mrs Ma, Hilda's mother. All the Mansfields call her Ma and he of course thinks it is her name.

Since the advent of the railway ten years earlier Farina had been enjoying something of a boom. Originally called Government Gums, its new name (from the Latin *farina,* flour) reflected hopes prevalent at the time that the region would prove suitable for wheat growing, although it was well north of the line which the Surveyor General, Goyder, had set as the limit for agriculture, because of unreliable rainfall. It had quickly become an important service centre and trucking point for livestock, wool and copper ore. With a population of around 600, it should have afforded Edward a modest living. But the drought of the early 1890s had not only meant poor wheat harvests: it had affected the town's other activities as well. On 6 April 1893 Nellie wrote to her sister Emma:

> It has been raining here all the morning and I do think it means it this time. It has been fearfully dry and everything very quiet in consequence. Teamsters have been obliged to stop carting; some of them started weeks ago with stores for different stations and each had to turn back, on account of there being no water for their horses, and a great many of them lost their best teams through thirst. However, people are beginning to think that the drought has broken up now, and I hope it has.

Whether because of the drought or for other reasons, Edward was apparently not doing well, for he kept making inquiries about openings elsewhere. The Ferry family were apparently also concerned for him to move to a better practice, for Emma sent him word that she had heard there might be an opening for him in Petersburg (the Peterborough of today), but he found on making inquiries that there was no substance to the rumour. A chance to move finally came in December 1893, in the form of an offer from the Queensland government: there was a post for a doctor in Birdsville, a little town in Queensland just twelve kilometres beyond the South Australian border. Nellie was jubilant: 'We will be six days getting there by coach,' she wrote to her mother, 'but as there is a salary of £2-0-0 at the end of it I don't mind, to say nothing of their having accepted the doctor's papers in Brisbane, and once registered there, it will hold good in any of the colonies, which is a great consideration.' She added that Edward had been in correspondence with Birdsville and other places for about a year, but Birdsville had made the best offer.

Nellie had been counting the weeks till Christmas, which they had planned to spend with her parents at Napperby near Port Pirie, but explained to her mother that they would not be coming after all:

> We intend leaving for Birdsville in about a fortnight's time and it will take me all my time getting ready, and besides we shall want all the money we can screw together for expenses. etc . . . Although they have allowed £20 travelling expenses, it will cost us a great deal more to get everything up.

She went on to tell her mother everything she had heard about Birdsville:

> There is a Chinaman's garden, a river (fish in it), three hotels, three stores, customs house (two officers), three policemen, police magistrate, and as far as we know, the house we are to occupy has four rooms, detached kitchen, bathroom, and underground tank; and mail comes from Hergott once a week.

Pussy was still with her Aunt Emma in Port Pirie and an immediate problem was how to get her up to Farina in time for their departure. Fortunately, at the last moment family friends, Mrs Mansfield (Frank's 'Ma') and her daughter, were able to bring her up on the train on 22 December. (One good turn deserves another and exactly a month later, when Mrs Mansfield was returning from Broken Hill to Port Pirie by train, Nellie's eldest sister sent the following note to her brother Jack, who was the station master at Caltowie on the Broken Hill line: 'Dear Lena and Jack. Kindly look out for Mrs Mansfield tomorrow afternoon's train for P.P., refreshing them with cups of tea if not too much inconvenience. Love to all, Emma Pearce for Mrs Ferry.'

Nellie describes Pussy's arrival in Farina in a letter to her sisters:

> The little dear . . . had eyes for nobody but Frank. She was full of the things that different aunties had made her. Mrs Mansfield bought her a doll and Frank a train in Quorn and the first thing she said was, Frankie, this train is for you and there are such a lot of cherries in the basket for you, Mother, Grand-mother sent them. This was all said in one breath, but the pretty thing did not think much of Farina and I admired her taste.

The children by now were aged four, three and seven months.

Pussy's 'box', with all her clothes in it, had gone astray on the journey up, but turned up the following day, fortunately, since they were to depart for Birdsville that evening.

> You can imagine how thankful I was. As it was, I got up at four o'clock and made several pairs of draws [sic] before seven, in case the box did not turn up before we left . . . I cannot thank you enough for all you did for Puss and especially the sewing. It was so nice to have everything made up instead of having to rush and make things.

That evening they travelled by train over the short stretch from Farina to Hergott, their starting point for the six-day coach journey up the Birdsville Track. Hergott or Herrgott, named after David Herrgott, the discoverer of the nearby springs, a member of John McDouall Stuart's party on his second expedition in 1859, is the present township of Marree. The name was changed by act of the South Australian Parliament during the First World War, when anti-German feeling was running high. After the railway line was extended to Hergott it became important as a supply base for the region, and the trucking point for livestock arriving on the hoof down the Track, as well as a base for cameleers transporting goods all over northern South Australia.

Here Edward and Nellie and their little family arrived at nearly midnight, making it a long day for Nellie after her 4 a.m. start to sew Pussy's 'draws' that morning. They had to be up again at four-thirty the next morning to set off for Birdsville. The hotel at which the family slept those few hours, Marree's only hotel, is still standing, very little changed, though the Afghan camel drivers no longer congregate with their teams outside it.

2

Buggy Ride to Birdsville

The Birdsville Track in 1893 took much the same route as it does today. It had been opened up only about twenty years earlier to bring cattle, bred in the Northern Territory and Gulf Country and fattened in the so-called Channel Country of south-west Queensland, down to the nearest railhead. Originally this was Port Augusta, but the line was extended in 1882 to Farina, and in 1884 to Hergott. Birdsville, although on the Queensland side of the border with South Australia, is much nearer to Adelaide than to Brisbane, 1200 kilometres distant, as against 1600 kilometres.

Before the South Australian Government put down artesian bores at intervals of about 48 kilometres along the Track in the early years of this century, the Track followed the Diamantina River down to the Derwent River, then at Cowarie Station swung south-east to Mungerannie, so that stock could take advantage of whatever surface water was to be had. The bores at Mirra Mitta and Mount Gason were to enable stockmen to take the much shorter route, Clifton Hills – Mount Gason – Mirra Mitta – Mungerannie, the length of the Track being either 490 kilometres or 564 kilometres, depending on whether the normal route along the bed of the Diamantina or the longer flood route was followed. Travellers had to take the longer route if there had been any recent rain south of the town of Winton in central Queensland. The coach on which the Hoche family travelled took the longer route via Cowarie, and they covered this distance by mail coach and open buggy in exactly six days. Not bad going, if you consider that even as recently as the 1960s the mail truck took three days for the trip. (These days you can make it, road conditions permitting, in one day of hard driving, although the tourist pamphlets advise allowing two days.) Since 1970 the Birdsville mail has been carried by air.

The Birdsville Track has been described as 'no more than a nebulous sense of direction',[7] and up until the 1970s this was a pretty accurate description. Afghan cameleers, whose long strings of camels in the early days brought all heavy loads up and down the Track, sought to aid their sense of direction by building huge cairns of stones at intervals along stretches of featureless plain; some of them can still be seen from the Track, though with green cover they look like small hills. Where the track was discernible at all it was just two parallel ruts, but over vast stony sections the surface was too hard for ruts to be formed, while elsewhere they vanished under dunes or drifting sand.

In the 1970s the Track was greatly improved, to enable stock to be transported by road train rather than on the hoof. Though its surface still alternates between rutted mud and jarring stones, there is evidence that a grader has been over it, and South Australian Highways Department machines can be seen working to further improve the worst sections. Some short stretches have been relocated over better ground.

But back to the year 1893. All were up at 4.30 a.m. on 24 December, to get away in the coach by 7.a.m. In a letter to her family after their arrival in Birdsville, Nellie describes the loading up of the coach:

> Frank was walking about with his train parcel under his arm and my basket in his hand, telling everyone he met that it was his luggage for Birdsville and when the coachman was loading up he marched up to him and said, Will you put my luggage up, too, please, it's for Birdsville. Of course, everyone laughed, and the coachman said, Young man, I am going to chuck it away. Poor little Frank's lip went down and he said, You mustn't, my grandmother gave me that train. So the driver said, Alright

little chap, we will find a safe place for it. Then Frank turned round to me and said, It's rude to say chuck isn't it, mother, and he and the driver were friends from that moment.

Nellie's letter goes on:

It was an awfully close morning, and the motion of the coach made us feel quite seasick, and at about 11 o'clock poor little Frank had turned quite queer and fainted right away twice. Then the Dr took him in front of the coach and he got alright and came along all the way splendidly and arrived here better than anyone of us, but you can imagine what a turn it gave me, especially as he has been so well. But the Dr said it was just the same as being seasick. We had a bottle of brandy with us in case of bad water so it came in nicely for him, mixed with lime juice. He thought it very nice medicine.

At 12 o'clock we arrived at the Clayton Bore, a hot spring. The water was rushing out at the rate of 50 000 gallons a day, and was too hot to bare our hands in, but such beautiful fresh water we filled up all the water bags.

This must have been a bore put down by an early pastoralist, because the government bore at Clayton was not put down till 1908. Later travellers have described the artesian water of the bores as rather saline, with an aperient effect, and some are said to have added citric acid to it to counteract the taste of washing soda. These days a thick green algal scum on the surface of the cooling pond does not entice the traveller to sample it, with or without additives.

Nellie goes on:

We then drove again and reached the Clayton Waterhole, a beautiful place, at half past three, had dinner at an eating house, changed horses, started at six o'clock the same evening and drove 35 miles to a place called Blaze's Well. And, my dears, I can assure you I thought we had come to blazes sure enough, but altered my opinion when we got up next morning and saw a beautiful sheet of water right in front of the house, with pelicans and spoonbills and all sorts of birds swimming in it.

The next morning, Christmas Day, they were on the road again a few minutes after six and about half past eleven reached the Kopperamanna outstation of the Lutheran Mission on Lake Killalpaninna. Nellie writes:

> Two blacks came out, dressed in white, and brought two bottles of goat's milk for the children to drink, besides a jugful for us. It was such a pretty place, and there were hundreds of those pretty pink and grey cockatoos flying about in the trees, screaming enough to deafen us.

Today all that remains of this pretty place, with its Aborigines dressed as waiters offering milk to travellers, are remnants of the wooden frames of some of the mission's mudbrick buildings. These sad skeletons, made from stunted and twisted tree trunks or branches, prop each other up amid the rabbit-infested sand dunes at the edge of the lake. There are numerous clumps of reeds but not a blade of grass within miles.

The Kopperamanna mission, 145 kilometres north of Marree, was established on a lake of that name in early 1867 as a mission to the Dieri Aborigines by a small group of Moravian Brethren from Victoria. They collaborated in their work with a Lutheran mission established at the same time at Lake Killalpaninna, sixteen kilometres away, which was supported by two South Australian synods with help from Hermannsburg in Hanover. But very soon after they were founded the missions began to experience the effects of long and devastating droughts, and by 1873 the discouraged Moravian Brothers had withdrawn. Kopperamanna was then taken over by the Lutherans and when the whole enterprise was reorganised in 1878, under the name Bethesda, Kopperamanna was made its outstation.

From 1869 the two missions were jointly run as a sheep station, with a herd of goats for meat, milk and cheese, and a few cattle. A village or hamlet grew up at Bethesda, its buildings constructed of mudbricks made with clay and rushes. Besides a church and a schoolroom, there were separate houses for the missionaries and their lay helpers, kitchens and accommodation for Aborigines.

Ruins of the Kopperamanna Mission

Varying numbers of the Dieri tribe lived at or near the mission, which distributed government rations as well as providing religious instruction and schooling. Numbers of them were employed on the station, though the Lutherans found their habit of going 'walkabout' disconcerting, for in good seasons the Aborigines tended to revert to traditional foods and did not bother to collect their mission rations.[8]

Good seasons brought up the annuals, providing abundant feed for stock, and water for vegetable gardens. The lakes filled, attracting birds and fish. But from the early 1890s the good seasons also brought rabbits in their millions, as well as thousands of dingos to prey not only on them but on the mission's goats and sheep. In bad seasons the pests died alongside their prey, the lakes dried up and pelicans flocked to feed on the fish stranded in the dwindling water.

The mission sheep station seems to have been the only one on the Track to remain in operation continuously right up to World War I, because the generous contributions of the Lutheran congregations backing it saw it through years of drought that forced all its neighbours off the land. The Hoche family saw it when times were good, for it reached the peak of its prosperity and success in the 1890s. But three years after they passed that way Kopperamanna, too, commenced a period of decline from which it never recovered. Starting with the drought of 1897, in which it lost 22 000 of its 28 000 sheep,[9] it struck a series of seasons so bad that even the resource and industry of its pastors, their long-suffering wives and devoted lay helpers, supplemented by the financial contributions of the faithful, could not save it. It was sold in 1915 to a Lutheran Pastor Bognor and his partner, though the Bethesda schoolteacher stayed on until 1917, when the government closed the mission school, along with all other Lutheran schools in South Australia. In 1920 the station was sold again, this time to a returned soldier, who in turn was eventually driven out by drought. The mission ruins today are on what is now the Etadunna cattle station.

Back on the Track, near Etadunna homestead, where once stood the Mission shearing shed with stands for sixteen sheep, a tall, austere steel cross has been erected, bearing two plaques which commemorate the work of the Lutheran missionaries. One was placed there in 1967, on the anniversary of the mission's founding; the second in 1986, on the 150th anniversary of the founding of South Australia.

The coach travellers were only given a half hour's rest at Kopperamanna and then were on the road again, reaching the Cooper River for dinner. Nellie writes:

> Such a beautiful place. The blacks came around in dozens, made our fire, boiled the billy, two went off to catch fish, others caught the fresh horses, and when we were just beginning our dinner (all spread out under the trees) two surveyors came along and joined us and we had quite a picnic. But I was so sorry, the

blacks came along with the fish just as we were ready to start, and we didn't taste them. They were such beauties, too. Puss and Frank took their dolls out to show the blacks. Oh, I wish you could have seen them. Some ran away screeching, others laughed. It was such fun, and Master Frank waxed quite brave and chased them with his.

The 'blacks' were not there just by chance. The mail contractors kept fresh horses for the coach at frequent intervals along the route, in the charge of Aboriginal stockmen, and it was with them that the travellers picnicked and camped overnight when there were no more station owners to welcome them.

Nellie's letter to her family goes on:

There were some beautiful flowers growing on the sandhills near the Cooper. In fact, they were like a garden. You know the flower we call pincushions, well, they were there in hundreds, also a pretty little shrub growing close to the ground, with flowers exactly the same as your meranda, only blue, and the leaves were different. Then there was another beautiful thing—a shrub—it looked like a sunflower in the distance. But instead of the leaves being coarse they were just like velvet, and the flower was exactly like the Sturt pea, only yellow. Oh, if this pen were only a speller, I might be able to describe everything, but as it ain't, I can't. The driver said the flowers are nothing now to what they are in the spring, and told me that the things will not grow away from their native soil. You can't imagine anything like the sandhills, they are just a blaze of bloom, and the sand is so hot we could not bear to touch it. The driver stopped several times and let the children pick them.

It is hard to identify this land of flowers and shimmering lakes and this Cooper River teeming with fish with the desolate and waterless region where the explorers Burke and Wills perished; hard to believe that this is the rough and treacherous Birdsville Track, where over the years people and even whole mobs of cattle have vanished in sandstorms or died of heat and thirst. As recently as December 1963 five members of an English family named Page perished there from thirst. They had not taken the precaution of notifying the authorities of their movements and when their car broke down rescue came too late. (These days it is hard to find anyone to notify of your intention to go up the Track, for if you go to the Marree police station to do so you will be greeted by a notice on the door announcing 'Police absent', and advising you to contact the police at Leigh Creek. Leigh Creek is 113 kilometres to the south!)

The Hoche family, too, were travelling in December, at the height of summer, when the temperature in the shade is frequently above 40°C for days on end. But they had the good fortune to strike a good season. A drought had just broken, and 1893–94 is recorded as a year of moderate but well-distributed rainfall. But in this country the effects of rainfall do not last. The evaporation rate is 100 inches a year, compared with an average rainfall of five inches or, as the explorer Cecil Madigan preferred to describe it, ten inches a year or nothing.[10] The perennials such as salt bush on which permanent stocking depends have virtually been wiped out along the Track by overstocking and constant grazing in the days when both sheep and cattle were brought down on foot to market. The good seasons are few and far between, as witness Madigan's story of how, on revisiting Lake Eyre in 1939, he found his own tyre tracks of ten years before, almost as clear as the day he made them.[11]

On Christmas night, Nellie's letter goes on, the coach party reached Two Wells. (She may have been confusing Two Wells with New Well.) She writes:

We dined off wild turkey, ham, plum pudding and Christmas cakes in plenty. It was a German's place, so we were in town. We were up and off early next morning, had dinner at an eating house by a large water hole, full of camels and Afghans, then restarted for Cowarie head station. Arrived there at half past twelve at night, just about used up. Mrs Helling, the owner's wife, got up and gave us a fine supper, and we turned into a nice airy bedroom, real glad to lie down. The children used to go to sleep about sundown, and I would undress them, so that it was only a matter of putting them into bed. The driver said that in the whole eight years he had been driving on that road he had never driven such good children . . .

The German settler, August Helling, in whose house the travellers spent the night, had taken up Cowarie Station in 1875, and it was he who had established this mail and passenger service by coach from Hergott to Birdsville in 1886.[12] The journal of the Birdsville Police Sergeant McDonald for 10 April 1886 recorded the arrival of the first mail coach in Birdsville at 6.p.m. from Adelaide, 'four good horses and a two-wheeled coach, with two horses in the shafts. Looks a very strong affair. Mr Ellon [Helling], the owner, came with the coach. No passengers for here. Two returned to Adelaide next morning by the coach.'[13] Helling later discarded his two-wheeled coach for a fully-fledged Cobb & Co. model but, according to outback chronicler, George Farwell, found it 'too cumbersome, as the hamper-top gave it too much wind-resistance, so he stripped it off, his passengers having to endure the full blaze of the sun. Later, buggies and wagonettes were found more effective.'[14] Mails in the early 1880s had been carried by packhorse and, until 1884, over a different route, from Farina to Cowarie, where they were exchanged for mail from Birdsville.[15] Stories of drivers who over the years got the mail up and down the Birdsville Track by horse, coach or truck, despite heat, sandstorms, gibbers, flies, mud and flood have become legend.

'At Cowarie', Nellie writes, 'we changed coaches and drivers, and continued our journey in an open trap, a great improvement on the little box of a coach.' Nellie never complained that anything was unpleasant or uncomfortable until there had been a change for the better, so she did not complain of the 'little box of a coach' until the change was made to the open trap, just as

Koonchera Sandhill after rain. Birdsville Track.

she had not complained about Farina until Pussy, seeing it for the first time on the eve of their departure for Birdsville, said she did not think much of it, and Nellie 'admired her taste'. She goes on:

> The horses all along the road were splendid ones, and we drove five in hand. The starting was always a bit lively. The horses were put in with the hobbles on, and they were not taken off until everything was ready and the driver was in the box. Then the blackboys quietly took them off, and such a prancin' and buckin' I never see. We used to change horses three times a day on account of the dreadful roads.

After leaving Cowarie the party had yet another change of horses and had lunch beside a very pretty waterhole, full of little water hens.

It was at this place that we saw the first of the naked blacks, and they were *stark staring* naked, with the exception of the men, and they wore a simple string round their waists with a sort of tassel in front, awful pretty. These were terribly afraid of the dolls, so I got the children to put them away. Well, we started off again, and passed some very pretty country. But don't suppose for a minute that we didn't see some awful dreary country as well. For instance, we drove through a plain, thirty miles as flat as a floor, with nothing but small stones and saltbush.

(This would have been a stretch of Sturt's Stony Desert, which is covered by shiny reddish stones, or gibbers.)

We stopped in a creek for dinner, changed horses, and were caught in a heavy thunder storm. The driver fixed up a sort of tent over the trap and we did not get wet at all. After this we drove 28 miles, pitched *a real tent*, and camped out. The blacks made our fire, boiled the billies and made baby's food. All we had to do was to eat our tea and turn in. It was fine fun and the youngsters thoroughly enjoyed it.

We were off in the morning at 7 o'clock and reached Goyder's Lagoon for dinner. Had dinner at a station. The manager was home. He was such a nice man—his name was Turnbull. He was delighted with the children, brought them a whole lot of puppies and kittens to play with, and did all in his power to make things comfortable. In fact, he got the driver to stay two hours longer than usual, which was very fine, then off again, horses prancin' and kickin', youngsters sorry. Then we passed the Goyder's Lagoon, a splendid sheet of water seven miles long, full of wild ducks. Then came the aforesaid plain, and after that camp and bed.

Next day we reached Andrewilla police station, a pretty little spot, with two log huts. Two policemen and their wives live there. [This was the South Australian customs post and border control.] They were so kind, especially the women. They seemed as though they could not do enough for me, made tea and made us a grand lunch. I was really sorry I was not hungry, as it is only once in a while that they see a white woman. I felt sorry to leave them. Off again, reached Katakuna for dinner. [She means Karathunka, a waterhole on the Eleanor River; she had difficulty spelling it and writes 'got him after a struggle, pretty nigh broke my pen'.] And lo and behold, the mail horses had got away and the blacks could not find them so we had to make the best of it and wait. They turned up just as the sun was going down and we had thirty miles to go to reach this beautiful city. Well, we did it, and our horses knocked up seven miles from here, and it took us nearly three hours to come that distance. The consequence was we reached Birdsville a few minutes after one in the morning, just about used up. The children were all asleep and so did not make much trouble. Thank goodness the people at the hotel we stopped at got up and made us tea, and were very kind.

Nellie's account of this trip along the Birdsville Track, with its eating houses, staging posts, police posts, missions and numerous stations gives the impression that the Track region was much more closely settled than it is today. And this is true. There were fifteen to twenty stations along the Track in the 1890s, for the settlement of this region was quite recent, and the settlers had not yet realised the limitations of the strictly marginal lands. The first of them had pushed north of the Flinders Ranges in the early 1860s, in the footsteps of the explorers, Eyre, Sturt and McDouall Stuart. The glowing accounts of the country along the Cooper brought back by the search parties for Burke and Wills, particularly that led by McKinlay, quickened interest in land in that area. They had struck a good season and found it a country of meadows and pastures. By 1881 leases had been taken up in the extreme north-east corner of South Australia; and though there had been years of bad drought, the good seasons were so good that new settlers were always ready to tackle holdings abandoned in despair a short time before. There was a serious drought as early as 1864–66, severe enough to warrant the establishment of a Drought Commission in 1867, but it was followed by over a decade of fairly good seasons, and would-be settlers thought the evidence before the Drought Commission had been exaggerated. More and more leases were taken up, and with the fat cattle pouring down from over the Queensland border, (14 000 head of cattle and 12 000 sheep passed the Kopperamanna Mission in one three-month period), the Track was a settled and busy place.

But by the turn of the century, when the worst drought since Australia was settled by Europeans closed every station along the Track, the grim realities of this country were being realised. One reasonably good season in five was not enough. The annuals which come up in such abundance after the rains fatten the stock but the permanent stock-carrying capacity of the country depends on the drought-resistant perennial shrubs which are slow to regenerate and easily destroyed.

As these limitations of the country have come to be realised, after a bitter history of astronomic stock losses and of stations abandoned time and again, the pattern of settlement in this region has changed. No longer is there much sign of the human activity which characterised the Track in the 1890s, though at Mungerannie, 206 kilometres up the track from Marree, a roadhouse offers petrol, food and drink, even an overnight stay. There are fewer stations, and although the names of these appear on signposts along the way, few of the actual homesteads are visible from the Track.

Cattle, not sheep, are grazed north of the dingo fence, which runs 9 600 kilometres from the Great Australian Bight in South Australia to Jimbour in south-eastern Queensland, crossing the Track north of Lake Harry, about 42 kilometres north of Marree. Under the state's soil erosion act, limits are set to grazing, to prevent further deterioration of the perennials. Some station owners have other properties in different parts of the country and are able thus to ride out bad years along the Track. Their daily lives, or those of their resident managers, have grown more comfortable: all stations have artesian bores which, in addition to giving them abundant water, enable them to generate electricity, with all the extra comforts which that brings; some own planes; some use helicopters for mustering; one has a speed boat parked alongside its four-wheel-drive vehicles, ready for use on the Cooper River, and since June 1991 all have been linked to the world outside by satellite telephone. All in all, life on the Track is very different from how it was when the Hoche family passed along it a hundred years ago.

3

Town in the Middle of Nowhere

Birdsville is still, as it was in the 1890s, the most isolated town in Australia, set in a treeless expanse of sand, over 300 kilometres from the nearest town. The temperature in summer can be as high as 49°C for days on end. While the average annual rainfall is 127 millimetres, in times of drought there can be no rain at all for years on end; but if there are good rains to the north the town can be floodbound for months by the waters of the Diamantina River.

It is not surprising, then, that the population these days is small, about fifty whites and some twenty resident Aborigines, while other Aborigines come and go. There are a hotel, a motel and a mission hospital, and in the 1960s the main road through the little town was paved with bitumen, all 100 metres of it, and given a nature strip down the centre. An artesian bore provides an abundance of hot water and a turbine has harnessed its power to provide the town with electricity. Both the Track and the town have become tourist attractions, their very isolation being their claim to fame, and tourist buses are often parked outside the hotel where once the stagecoach drew up. Frequently a plane can be seen parked nearby. The town's main tourist attraction is the annual race meeting. In an interview on ABC national radio on 6 September 1991 the local police sergeant said he was expecting around 5 000 people for the races who, on past experience, would arrive on some 250 flights. The festivities, including a ball, would last for a week!

But in 1893 Birdsville was a new little town and, though it was flourishing, living conditions were primitive in the extreme. Originally known as the Diamantina Crossing, it grew up around a store established in 1882 by a station owner named Frew to enable drovers bringing cattle from the stations to the north to stock up with supplies before starting on the long trek to Hergott. It was officially laid out on its present site in 1885, so it was only eight years old when the Hoche family arrived there. But being located near Queensland's rich Channel Country, at the head of what was at that time the most important main stockroute in Australia, it had quickly grown into a sizeable township. It had a population in the 1890s of around 90 whites in the town, plus about 180 Aborigines, with an estimated 130 more whites in the surrounding district, working on stations or on the construction of a fence along the South Australian/Queensland border. It was important not only as a supply depot, but as a police station and as the Queensland customs post for the South Australian border. The town itself was a wild place and the police, with jurisdiction over an area of 77 700 square kilometres, were kept busy dealing with cattle thieves and smugglers out to trick the customs, as well as organising search parties for people lost in the desert.

The police officers seem to have taken everything in their stride, as their reports indicate: Journal note of Sergeant Arthur McDonald: 'January 22 1889: Sub-Inspector Sharpe shot himself on the police station verandah this afternoon. Another hot day.' And the police report of Senior Constable A. Scarlett for 3 May 1894: 'A Dennett, Manager of Rosebery Station, will not part with the rifle that J.H. Barnard committed suicide with, being the only rifle on station and wanted for station use.'[16]

It was the job of the customs officers in these pre-Federation days to levy taxes not only on all station supplies but on all cattle going south, the charge being £1 and later £2 a head. In 1894 a

Mr Edward Ward seems to have led a busy life as police magistrate and officer-in-charge of border customs, as well as acting land commissioner and land agent. There were also a police sergeant and one or more constables, and about twenty black trackers, all with horses or camels. A list of the trades, professions and clubs of the town in *Pugh's Almanac* for 1894 gives as nice and complete a picture of Birdsville at that time as you could wish for. There was an aerated water manufacturer, an auctioneer, a blacksmith, two booksellers, two builders, a butcher, a medical man, a saddler, two storekeepers, a cricket club, two jockey clubs, a lawn tennis club, and three hotels, the Birdsville, the Royal and Tattersalls.[17]

It is not known which hotel the Hoche family stayed at, but the journal of the local police sergeant at that time contains constant references to disorderly conduct, fighting, gambling, drunkenness and 'shocking language' in all three. Perhaps it was just as well that the family moved into their house the very next day or Frank might have added stronger words than 'chuck' to his vocabulary of 'rude' words.

Nellie dashed off a letter to her mother the following morning, so it could go with the coach on its return journey. She told her they had arrived safely but, still mindful of her mother's insistence that letters be well written, added:

> I am not going to write you about the journey until we are settled, and if I can get a pen as will spell well, will give you a full description next time. We have got a four roomed house furnished for 11/- per week, and are going into it this afternoon.

She thanked her sister Emma again for all she had done for Puss, and for the sewing and parcel, adding:

> Little Puss just said tell grandmother about the blacks without clothes on, we saw hundreds of them. You must excuse this hurried note but we are all so unsettled, you know just how we are, but will try and write a decent letter next week.

Iron house of the period, Marree

Some days later Nellie wrote a much longer letter to her younger sisters, describing their first days:

On the morning after our arrival, we got up, had a look around, heard about this house and took it. It is a three roomed iron house, broad verandah all round, detached kitchen and washhouse, furnished. The bedroom has a large cedar wardrobe with five draws [sic] at the bottom. Big chest of draws, double washstand, dressing table, big oval mirror, and a real swell bedstead, brown and brass commode, real beauty; no carpet of any sort. The sitting room [has] a big wooden sofa, oval cedar table, big deal table, [unreadable] chair and a whole dose of very good pictures. Kitchen—nice large safe and table, so when our things arrive, which I suppose they will by a team in six or seven weeks from now, I shall be in town. Until then we are having our meals in a hotel. They only charge £2 per week for all of us, and I am beginning to think that it will be cheaper for us than housekeeping, or cooking for ourselves, as things are

Transferring mail en route to Cordillo Downs Station. c. 1920

terribly dear. Only fancy, flour sixpence per lb., sugar eightpence, jam 2/- per tin, bread 1/- per loaf. I bought two small wash-tubs yesterday and paid 28/- for them. The Customs Officer, Mr Ward, and his family board at the hotel and live at their own house. They say it is cheaper and saves killing themselves in the heat cooking ... We were at the chinaman's garden on Sunday. He has a fine garden and sells his grapes for 1/6d per lb, water melon 1/6 each, pretty stiff eh? There are two other gardens besides, but they all charge the same, the devils, so taking everything into consideration, I reckon taking our meals will be cheaper for us, as we get fruit every day ... Well my dear old girls, this pen is beginning to jib so will have to stop. You will be pleased to hear that we are all in good health, and the old man has had a good many patients. Will tell you more about Birdsville when I know myself. It is a much prettier place than Farina.

In this letter Nellie also mentions a strange coincidence:

Oh I must tell you that I have met a Miss Ferry, she is governess at Wards, and strange to say she is one of fourteen. Ain't that strange? And there were seven boys and seven girls, so when she told me that I says shure you must be a relation, for our family has just the same number. But she is Irish and says we are the first Ferrys she has ever heard of outside their own family. She comes from N.S.W. Anyhow, I swear she must be a relation.

Despite Nellie's quaint assumption, Marie Louise Ferry was no relation of her family, though her Christian names suggest French origins (Nellie's father's family came originally from French-speaking Flanders). In 1899 Marie Louise was appointed the first teacher of the Birdsville Provisional School, only to resign barely two months later when the three months' sick leave she had applied for was refused. She was to die later in Birdsville and was buried there.[18]

Nellie was not to get a chance to tell her family more about Birdsville, for only five weeks after their arrival she came down with typhoid fever. Edward's letters to her family indicate that from the moment they got there he had been kept busy treating typhoid cases, both in Birdsville and in outlying districts, some well over 150 miles from the town. However, in a letter written on 10 February to Nellie's eldest sister, Emma Pearce, Edward writes that so far her case seems to be only mild. But he adds: 'I could not vouch for anything final as I had very disappointing results from cases of a similar nature during our stay here.'

In the absence of a town water supply, sanitary conditions must have been poor and the possibilities of treatment were certainly limited. Edward went on:

It is impossible to get anything in the way of comforts, no champagne within 130 miles, ice out of the question. Even it is impossible to get an india-rubber to refit a selsogene [soda syphon]. In the same time people are very good with supplying milk, which is very scarce just now. Two hotels keep their own people without it. Mr Ward even took the trouble to send a circular round the different stations for milking cows to be sent in. I hope to be able to get champagne for Nellie on Friday next from the nearest place from here; a blackboy went with a note two days ago ... There is no kerosene to be got here for the last three weeks and you can very well imagine what miserable nights I have had of it with light of bad candles. It is only the last week that I have been able to read and write at all and then only in daytime. I had a very bad touch of sandy blight for the fortnight before.

Although other typhoid patients were put into isolation in Frew's store, Edward nursed Nellie himself at home. The midsummer heat in that little iron house must have been unbearable. The Wards were marvellously helpful. Edward wrote:

> Little Lennie is staying with the Wards and off [sic] course causes a certain amount of trouble through being weaned by force. Frank and Puss sleep at home but are all day away to keep the house quiet ... Little Frank and Puss are dear little children. They only see their mother 2x times daily, after being dressed and going to breakfast and in the evening at going to bed. Frank is getting quite fat, he eats as if he could not get enough; little Puss as usual acts mother to him. [Edward concludes on a reassuring note] If everything runs with Nellie as it is doing now, I hope to have her out of bed in a fortnight's time but of course it is impossible to tell. At all events you will hear from me with every mail.

On the back of this letter is written: 'Pussy's love, her mark' and a cross, and 'Frank's love, his mark', followed by his cross.

A week later Edward was able to report to Emma Pearce that Nellie was making really good progress, adding:

> The fever is gone now for the last four days; off course she is very weak yet and will be for some time to come but I reckon that with care every danger is past. When I mentioned last week about disappointing cases, I ment [sic] to say that the fever takes quite a different run from what I saw in Pirie, to a

certain extent caused through the impossibility of getting what is generally called medical comforts. The little ones are getting on first class. Frank is as sturdy as you want to make him, Puss the same good little girl as ever and little Lennie likes his adopted mother better than the real one. Nellie read yours and Bella's letters herself today . . . Business affairs are going very well here; certainly the typhoid outbreak helped it along. Just now I have a very bad case in hand, besides 2 with great suspicions, and as far as I can see some more sickening for it.

He was able to add some good news:

This morning's mail I got notice back from Brisbane, that the Government accepted my papers for registration; that will please your mother anyway.

Any pleasure the Ferry family may have had from that news was short-lived, however, for the mail the following week brought word that Nellie had had a bad relapse. 'In fact', Edward told Emma Pearce:

I considered it my duty to tell her what chances I reckoned she had. Excuse my writing with pencil but there is no ink to be got in the township. I had three cases running the same way, everything going all right for 14 days, then a sudden turn. But I reckon to be able to get Nelly through, everything going right. This morning's mail (the weekly Adelaide) we had letters from Germany that my people are wanting Nelly and the children to come to Hamburg for a holiday and they sent the money for their passage and something to spare over. Well, Mrs Pearce, I hope Nelly will be right enough to have the trip, it would do her such a lot of good, but in the same time I am very frightened that it will be a case. Nelly is very lively just now with Mrs Ward and the children around her, but she is very, very low. If any new development occurs I will send a blackfellow to Hergott with a telegram, it will save three days on the mail. My dear Mrs Pearce, hope with me for the best.

Jane Elizabeth Ward

The next letter, in faint pencil, was from Nellie, also to her sister Emma:

> My dear old Emma, am just writing a line or two to let you know how well I am getting on. I have been without fever for the last five days, and this morning had some cornflour for the first time. I was awfully frightened when I found out I had typhoid, although ever since I came here I felt I would get it and could not shake the feeling off. Dear little baby is looking so well and is so fond of Mrs Ward. Oh Emma, only for her I never would have come through. She came and took him directly she knew I was ill, and has kept him ever since. Fancy the poor little chap having to be weaned. Yesterday afternoon he came on to the bed for the first time and he has quite forgotten his titty. I could have cried when he turned from me and put his arms out for Mrs W, but it shows she is good to him. I am awfully thin and weak but I will be alright. The

poor old man has had to do every bit of nursing himself. Yours and mother's letters arrived this morning; was so glad to get them. My hand is doing the jibbing trick. I hope to be up next week and able to write a decent letter but just write this bit to let you see how well I am. Lots of love to all, Nell.

And on the top she has written a message for her younger sisters: 'Tell the girls I defied the fever.'

We know that she did not believe what she wrote, for she then turned to Edward and told him what she wanted done with her few possessions: her fur cloak to go to her mother, her lace dress to one sister and to another her lace handkerchief (a present from Edward's family). The two older children were brought to say goodbye just twenty minutes before she died, on 24 February 1894. She was only twenty-seven.

Edward immediately sent word to her family by 'telegram', which went by black runner to Hergott in the hope of saving three days on the mail coach time. But it took twelve days to get there, and went from there to Port Pirie by electric telegraph. He said that he and the children, accompanied by Mrs Ward, would be coming south at once. On the back of the telegram Nellie's mother Emma has written to the son-in-law who was to send a reply: 'I don't think you can say anything further than bring the children along. This has come like a thunderbolt to us.'

Mrs Ward and the children did go south, and only just in time, a day before the Diamantina River came down in flood, a flood in which Mrs Ward's young brother-in-law was drowned while she was away, leaving a wife and three children only a little older than the Hoche children. When she and the children reached Marree, not in a coach this time but in an open buggy, they were met by Lena, the wife of Nellie's eldest brother, Jack. Jack himself was unable to leave his post at Caltowie, where he was station master, but Lena travelled two days each way by horse and cart and took baby Len home with her. Mrs Ward took the two older children on to their grandparents in Port Pirie.

Edward had to stay in Birdsville, as he explained in a letter to Nellie's mother, to care for typhoid cases in the surrounding district and await two confinements, one of them at the Andrewilla police camp in South Australia, fifty-four miles away. When he wrote, Andrewilla was cut off from him by water, though he thought they might be able to get through with a boat. He said that Mrs Ward usually attended any confinements if no doctor was available but she was not back yet so he would have to stay. Besides, any travel would depend on the state of the floodwaters. A great body of water would be down in three or four days, so they might not have any mail for three weeks or a month. That week's mail had only got through on packhorses.

He did not write again to the Ferrys giving details of Nellie's death until 16 April, nearly two months later, having in the meantime heard from them that Mrs Ward and the children had arrived safely in Port Pirie. He said, to explain his long delay in writing, that he had been away for three weeks seeing a typhoid case 130 miles away, at Moukira. It had been 'a very miserable trip, constant rains, most parts of the country flooded and boggy, clothes and rugs wet through, the horses knocking up, besides running short of rations.' In a message to one of Nellie's brothers he added: 'Lennie is right when he says that snake does not taste bad baked in the ashes.'

Edward then described Nellie's last days:

Poor little Nell had been getting on splendidly before the relapse came. She even had been sitting outside one evening on the verandah for a short time (off course, carried out) and it seemed to do her good. Unfortunately her courses started for the first time after Lenny was born, alarmingly strong, bringing with them diarrhoea, which soon changed into blood discharge from the bowels. You know what that means and the poor girl knew it herself too well. She tried her hardest to keep her spirits up and to dissuade me from my opinion of the end the case would take but I knew that no help was possible. She had a craving for champagne during the last fortnight of her illness, but there was none to be got here, all the three hotels having run out of it during January races. I sent a black boy to the nearest township, Betoota, 240 miles away, for some and he brought their whole stock, 2 bottles, but he came too late. Nellie had gone before. On the morning of her death she was quite lively for her weakness and wrote the letter for you. At about half past ten she suddenly collapsed and in about 20 minutes it was over. She had time enough to kiss the children goodbye, at least Puss and Frank, Lenny was away with Mrs Ward. She was quite conscious up to the last minute and her last words were about the children. She wants to have them taken to Germany as soon as baby is old enough for the sea trip. I wrote home to my people about the sad affair but have not received any answer yet, in fact it is rather too early for it . . . There are a good many of Nellie's as well as the children's clothes left here yet, but I only can send on little Frank's overcoat, and this by special favour as the mail driver is not supposed to carry any parcels just now on acc of the water.'

He enclosed the letter Nellie had written to her sister Emma on the day of her death and added: 'Mrs Ward was wrong when she told you that it was found between the pillows. Nellie wrote it in my presence and closed it up and I kept it ever since. I intended to take it with me when I was coming down.' And he concluded by asking how to arrange about money affairs, presumably money for the keep of the children.

Nellie was buried in Birdsville. In 1927 Frank went there to see if he could find her grave. Although wild donkeys had chewed up most of the wooden fence around the cemetery and the wooden crosses on the other graves, a separate little fence had been maintained around his mother's grave and its cross was still intact. An old man whom he described as 'one of the local dead-beats' had known Nellie, and throughout the years had taken care of her grave. Frank kept in touch with the man, sending him £5 from time to time, but in 1933 the letter with money he had sent was returned because the old man had died. When a friend visited Birdsville in 1962 Frank asked him to look for his mother's grave in the cemetery, but by then it had vanished with the rest.

Despite what seems to have been a fairly widespread typhoid epidemic, Nellie was apparently one of only four people in Birdsville to die of it. A letter from the Divisional Clerk, Diamantina Divisional Board (now Diamantina Shire), addressed to the Colonial Secretary, 4 May 1894, contains a full account of the epidemic and of measures taken to control it:

> I have to report . . . That typhoid fever has been prevalent in this town for some time, and although in the first Cases were from people that came to the town with the fever upon them, that Several residents were stricken with the fever resulting in fatal Cases in the Doctor's wife, and the half Caste Girl, and the other fatal Cases (two) from being contracted outside. I have further to report that the Divisional Board took every precaution to stamp out this fever, by renting an Old Store and having it fitted up for the reception of typhoid patients, two patients having been there for about Six Weeks and now nearly all right again. Further that the Board have taken steps to have all the Houses in the town thoroughly disinfected, with I am glad to report satisfactory results. No further Cases being reported to date.[19]

Enclosed with the letter was an account from Dr Hoche for twenty professional visits at £1/1/0 each, and two miles' mileage fee at 5/- per mile for each of these twenty visits, making a total of £31/0/0. The account was for attendance on the half-caste girl who had died of the fever, and the Divisional Clerk was seeking authorisation to pay it. (This account makes it clear that the £2 a week Nellie had told her family Edward would be earning was just a base salary, and that Edward was able to charge fees and mileage in addition.)

While the Divisional Clerk in his letter gave the Board sole credit for the measures taken to control the epidemic, Edward had stayed on in Birdsville until May and he probably knew more about controlling the spread of infectious diseases than most doctors in Australia at the time. In the final year of his medical studies he had travelled as ship's doctor on a German ship from Hamburg to New York and, after observing at first hand the high incidence of infectious diseases on ships plying the east coast of the United States, on his return wrote his final thesis on the prevention of infectious diseases on board ship. In it he makes the most detailed recommendations for the prevention and control of such diseases.

The epidemic does seem to have been effectively controlled, as only seven deaths from typhoid are recorded in Birdsville's register of deaths for the two-year period 1892 to 1894.[20] These were deaths in the town itself—no figures are available for surrounding districts. There may have been others among Edward's patients outside the town, for he had seemed to imply a number of deaths when he wrote to the Ferrys: 'I had very disappointing results in cases of a similar nature during our stay here.' There were 102 known deaths from the disease in the whole of Queensland in 1894. The steps taken by in Birdsville to control it were doubtless in line with new health legislation passed by the Queensland government following a record number of deaths from typhoid—542—in the year 1884.[21]

4

The German Connection

With the epidemic under control, and the two confinements presumably attended to, Edward did not linger in Birdsville and in May 1894 returned to Port Pirie. The promised registration as a medical practitioner in Queensland never came through, no doubt because his time in Birdsville had been so short. His name does not appear on the list of medical practitioners registered in Queensland in that decade, and Health Department records and *Pugh's Almanac* both show a Dr Milne (the previous incumbent) as the Birdsville medical officer in that year.

The glimpses we get of Edward from Nellie's letters are of an exemplary husband, devoted to his wife and children. He appears more closely involved with his children than perhaps many German husbands in those days. When Frank was just over two Nellie described him to her family as 'always trying to make boats and trains', and added: 'As soon as Edward comes into the house he does not get a moment's peace until he has made some paper boats or a whip for him.' When Frank was ill with severe bronchitis in Farina it was Edward who sat up with him two nights, and when Nellie came down with typhoid he nursed her at home himself. He seems to have been on friendly terms with her family, and during her illness kept them informed of her condition. Though his letters are rather formal—he addressed her oldest sister Emma as Mrs Pearce—that could be just his German stiffness and style, and he always concluded 'with best love to you all'. And he sent the first news of her illness not to her mother but to her sister Emma, asking her to find some 'easy' way of breaking it to her mother.

With the benefit of hindsight we may discern one or two hints that the Ferrys, Nellie's mother in particular, might have been more assiduous than Edward himself in seeking an opening for him in a good practice, as when Emma Ferry wrote to him in Farina about a possible opening at Petersburg; and his comment to Nellie's eldest sister when word came to him at Birdsville that Brisbane had accepted his papers for registration, 'that will please your mother anyway', seems to suggest there was more concern on the part of the Ferrys over his job situation than he himself felt.

Though Edward presumably returned to Port Pirie to be with his children, once there he did not make a home for them, but left them in the care of the Ferrys while he himself moved into a boarding house kept by a relative of theirs. It would doubtless have been impossible for a busy doctor to bring up three children on his own, and help from the Ferry family would, for once, have been hard to provide. Though Nellie's three younger sisters were unmarried, it would probably not have been considered proper for an unmarried girl to keep house for her brother-in-law.

Edward also faced the problem on his return to Port Pirie of resuming medical practice. Whatever had forced him to look beyond Port Pirie for patients after his marriage still apparently blocked his path. Though he made at least one attempt to find work elsewhere as a doctor, when assured there was work at one place he did not take it. This was in May, soon after his return to Pirie, when he wrote to a member of the German community in Sedan, 52 kilometres east of Gawler, inquiring about the possibility of practising there. The reply told him that although there were two doctors practising in Sedan, one a woman, the other an old man, neither was well liked. The largely German community in the area would welcome a German doctor, and if he were prepared to come without a financial guarantee the job was his. If he were to insist on a minimum guarantee of £200 they would have to advertise the job and he might not get it. The writer added: 'I should mention that none of the doctors practising in the district of Sedan are "duly qualified" ', so clearly the fact that Edward was not registered was still not a barrier to practice in lightly populated areas.

As far as we know he did not follow up the offer, choosing instead to stay in Port Pirie, perhaps to be near the two older children, who were with their grandparents there. (Since the children's return from Birdsville Lennie had remained with Nellie's eldest brother, Jack, and his wife, Lena, at Caltowie.) A little printed notice advised the town that Dr Hoche was available for consultation at Mr Trezona's chemist shop.

The next time we hear of him, just over a year later, he is dead, apparently by his own hand and in rather sordid circumstances. The Adelaide *Advertiser* of 6 June 1895 reported both his death, in Solomon Town (a suburb of Port Pirie), and an inquest held to determine the cause. Evidence had been given that the deceased had been suffering from influenza, and had complained to his friends of being unable to sleep. The medical evidence was that when two doctors saw him when he was on the point of death they had the impression that he had taken an overdose of morphia for the purpose of inducing sleep, and this was the verdict of the inquest jury, and the cause of death given on his death certificate.

The *Port Pirie Advocate and Areas News* of the same date, in a much longer account, carried evidence from a number of people. A few days before his death Edward had left the boarding house where he usually lived, and moved into the Railway Hotel. Hotel staff testified that he had been out all one night and had been served a fair amount of whisky and beer over the following two days. He had complained on the day before his death of feeling ill and said he thought he had a bad attack of influenza. Between 5 and 6 a.m. on the third morning a fireman acting as hotel keeper heard moans and groans from the doctor's room and found him breathing very heavily and unconscious. An engine driver staying at the hotel had seen him trying to vomit and in great pain. Two doctors had been called.

Next Mr Richard Trezona, a chemist, testified:

> I have supplied Dr Hoche with drugs; he often complained to me that he was unable to sleep at night; he told me two months ago he had never taken morphia and that he never would; the bottle produced (found in the deceased's clothes) is out of a medicine chest and contained compressed tablets of some description; he has not purchased either morphia or opium from me for himself nor any other drug that he could use to make away with himself; [I] have seen Dr Hoche very regularly for the last few months; he has been keeping very straight and has not been addicted to drink; he had been drinking last Wednesday, but was not intoxicated.

Since Edward had practised out of this chemist's shop, the chemist would have known him well.

Yet another witness was the proprietor of the private boarding house where Edward had been living, Mr George Ball, whose wife was a second cousin of Nellie's, though this was not mentioned in the press account. He said:

> Dr Hoche was living at my place for some time; [I] have never heard him threaten to make away with himself; he was in debt; he has left his medical instruments at my place. Hoche last came to my house on Wednesday night; he stayed a very little while and went away; he gave no reason for going away.

The two doctors called to give evidence, Drs Stewart and Carr, said they had given him an injection of apomorphine to make him vomit; had used the stomach pump but found nothing in the stomach; had pumped some strong coffee into the stomach and pumped it out again, and then pumped in an emetic. Dr Stewart said he had had no hope from the first, as Edward's stupor was so deep. He believed he had taken morphia to induce sleep, and did not think a post-mortem of any utility as the cause of death was sufficiently apparent. He concluded with the comment, surprising since others had given evidence that Edward had been in great pain, that 'morphia would not produce great pain, but the contrary'.

Because Nellie's father was old and ill, and her eldest brother, Jack, lived some distance from Port Pirie at Caltowie, it was her eldest sister Emma's husband, Alfred Pearce, who had the difficult and delicate task of breaking the news of Edward's death to his family in Hamburg. Nine days after the event he wrote to Edward's brother, Richard Hoche, enclosing press clippings from *The Advertiser* and *The Port Pirie Advocate and Areas News*:

> It is with feelings of the deepest regret that I address you for the first time to convey to you the sad news of the death of your poor

Edith, Lennie and Frank. c.1895

brother Edward which occurred here on the morning of June 3rd, and the duty of writing to you is made the more painful from the circumstances surrounding his death. I am writing to you that you may break the sorrowful news more gently to your father and sisters to whom it must be a great shock and with whom we desire to express our deepest sympathy and love. The more fully detailed particulars of our poor brother-in-law's end will be found in the newspapers which I am posting with this.

He told them he had been with Edward when he died and had given him a Church of England burial, and went on:

For the last two months we had seen very little of your brother, so that we cannot say how he had been faring, but about the end of February last he had made arrangements to visit Germany; . . . his eldest [child], Edith, was to accompany him, and everything was in readiness for the trip, but at the last moment he gave up the project without assigning any reason and to that we attribute the cause of his not seeing us as frequently as he had formerly done. When he was in Birdsville Edward contracted ague, caused no doubt from bad water and indifferent food, and he proposed taking a trip to see his home, with a view to recouping his health. So far there has been no letter or other writing found that throws any light upon his untimely end, nor has any will been discovered. It is but right I should tell you that my impression is poor Edward was very poor, his worldly possessions being a horse, saddle and bridle, his professional instruments and clothing. He has some book debts, but from what I can gather these are small in comparison with what he owes to different creditors.

Alfred concluded reassuringly: 'The little ones have been cared for just as if they were our own, and their tender ages save them from realising the great grief of being orphans.' (The photograph of the three children printed opposite was taken shortly after this, to be sent to the family in Hamburg, and three more desolate-looking little children can hardly be imagined.)

Edward had two brothers in Germany, one, Richard, a lawyer, the other, Ludwig, a doctor, and two sisters, Anna and Elise. All had written frequently to Edward ever since his arrival in Australia, imploring him to write, but had had almost no word from him. When he wrote to tell them of Nellie's death they had been eighteen months without news, and for over a

Hoche family 1899 (Edward's siblings)
Left to right: Ludwig, Richard, Anna and Elise

year after her death they again heard nothing. Edward's mother was suffering from what her family called 'acute melancholia' and frequently wrote page after page pleading with him for news, but in vain. He just piled up the letters and cards. His mother was to die just two weeks before the grim news from South Australia reached Hamburg.

All the Hamburg family knew was that he had married, had a family and was supposedly prospering in his new life. They had been sent a photograph of Nellie at the time of her marriage to Edward and had had at least one letter from her. Alfred Pearce's letter and the dry newspaper reports, coming after a long period without news of Edward, would have been shattering to the family, but at least the scandal was far away. In due course a small notice appeared in the *Hamburgischer Correspondent*: 'On 3 June my son, Dr. med. Edward Hoche, died after a short illness in Port Pirie S.A. Please share our silent grief. Prof. Dr. Hoche.'

A gracious reply to Arthur Pearce's letter was sent by Edward's lawyer brother, Richard, explaining he was writing for his father whose eyesight was poor, and thanking the Ferry family for all they had done for Edward and were doing for his children. There was no reference, either then or later, to the circumstances of Edward's death nor to his debts; just the comment that Edward had not informed them by letter of how he stood and what property he had.

Richard then made on his father's behalf an offer to contribute to the education of the children to the extent of £50 sterling a year, until each child had completed his or her eighteenth year, or until Pussie married. But it must be understood, he emphasised, that these payments would have to cease on the death of his father, now aged sixty-one. His sisters were heirs to their father's estate and would not be able to continue the payments. He and his brother had no claims on the estate, as they and Edward had had their share in their education, for which their father had paid.

Although his sisters, Anna and Elise or Lies, wrote reasonable

English, and Richard had studied English, he wrote in German to the Ferrys on this and later occasions, explaining that in business matters he wanted to be sure of making quite clear what the arrangements were. The letters were translated at the South Australian end, usually by Jack Ferry's German father-in-law, Ernst Siekmann; in his absence by a German watchmaker whom Jack knew. Richard kept rough copies of all his own letters, sewn by hand into a file made of brown paper.

It was decided after Ferry family discussions in Port Pirie that Nellie's father would be the children's guardian, but in view of his age (sixty-three) and poor health, and the distance he lived from both bank and post office (in the little town of Napperby), his eldest son, Jack, would act in practical matters on his behalf. The appropriate steps were taken, on cooperation with the public trustee, who showed a touching concern for the family, asking if the German grandfather would not be willing to remit the money to the relative concerned without his being legally appointed guardian and so save the expense of a legal appointment.

Nellie's brother Jack was a meticulous man, with a strong sense of duty and very firm views on what was right and wrong. Four months later, in October 1895, he decided it was time the family in Germany was told the truth about Edward in more detail. Just why is not clear. It cannot have been in the hope of getting some financial help for the children, for the Hoche offer of help had already been received. After some preliminary remarks about the children's health he wrote to Richard Hoche:

> Considering all things I have come to the conclusion that it is much the best that I should acquaint you as plainly as such a delicate matter permits of some of the circumstances connected with your late brother Edward's career as associated with our family and his wife, my late sister Nellie, particularly that portion, say, about the two last years of his life, which I gather from your frequent appeals to him for news you had no knowledge of. You have wrongly blamed the post service for letters etc. going astray, but it has been and is most reliable. At the same

time you had every reason for concluding as you did, seeing that you had no response to your many enquiries. The cause of this, doubtless, was that Edward was too ashamed of the condition to which he, through his neglect of excellent opportunity, had brought his whole affairs. For though notwithstanding he twice endeavoured to pass the S.A. medical examination and failed (his diploma was not recognised here) yet he was acknowledged to be a really good medical man, and in the other doctor in Port Pirie he had little opposition. Had he been only moderately careful of himself and his practice he could easily have obtained a good position.

My late dear sister must have known only too well how things were going but she was too loyal to make any sign. She stayed with her two children with our parents at Napperby, near Port Pirie, pending Edward's making a success at Farina. Carrying then their third child, Leonard, whom, dear little fellow, we have with us, her confinement approaching, she went to him there.

The child was only 10 months old [Jack was wrong here: Len was only seven months old] when Edward again thought fit to seek fresh fields, going to Birdsville, a six-day coach journey thru the bush, arriving there about 1 January '94. The poor girl contracted typhoid fever before the end of the same month and died by the end of February in that God-forsaken place, where there was neither good nursing nor diet, leaving the three dear little ones. (I enclose a map, which will give you an idea of the position of the place.) Even in that out of the way place there was, God bless her, a lady with a motherly heart whose kindness went the length of bringing them back over this awful journey. My dear wife went to Hergott [Marree] to meet them and they have been with us ever since.

Edward returned to Port Pirie about two months after the children, where he endeavoured once more to establish a practice. This, of course, was next to impossible then. The only event worthy of record between then and his decease was an attempt to arrange his own and Edith's [Pussie's] departure to Germany to you, but which for certain reasons, chiefly owing to his indebtedness, he was not permitted.

However, my mother and sisters (and my wife who went to Port Pirie to see them off) got Edith ready for the voyage—this was in March last—and on the day of sailing Edward could not be found. Therefore our people decided that Edith should not go. Edward put in an appearance two days later, and the result naturally was that as he could not give a satisfactory account of his action a very marked coldness was extended to him, broken only by the necessity of his attendance professionally upon my father during his illness.

It is with the greatest sorrow that I make these disclosures, as I judge from letters from the several members of your family that you were all deeply concerned about Edward's welfare.

He then referred to their kind offer to help with the children's education and assured them that the children were being well cared for, adding: 'Frank is the only delicate child and always has been, but all are wonderfully intelligent . . . My father-in-law, Mr Ernst Siekmann, once of Minden, went through Edward's papers and kindly translated all of importance.' (Each of the closely written letters and letter-cards has a one-line summary written in red across it, usually saying: 'From his family again, asking him to write.' Jack's wife, Caroline or Lena, was Ernst Siekmann's elder daughter.)

The Ferry family papers contain no response by the Hoches to Jack's letter, nor was there a copy of any reply in Richard's brown paper file. Given the habit of the families at both ends of this correspondence of keeping letters and in the case of Edward's brother Richard, copies of letters, it seems probable that no reply was sent.

If, as Jack Ferry reported to Edward's parents, he had twice failed in an examination because his German qualifications were not recognised, he probably sat for these examinations just before he went to Birdsville or just after his return, for it was only around the end of 1893, the date at which he left for Birdsville, that such examinations were introduced. (According to the Registrar of the Medical Board of South Australia, there is no record of any 'proving examination' being in existence under the 1880 or 1889 Acts, nor of the precise date of their introduction.)[22]

The riddle of Edward's conduct during his years in Australia is unlikely ever to be solved. Were it not for the German Consul's reference to his having 'sown wild oats' before he left

Nellie's brother Jack and wife Caroline

Germany, and his mention in his first letter to his family from Port Pirie to debts left behind him in Hamburg, one might well assume that he only went to pieces after Nellie's tragic death. If, as he claimed in his first letter home, he had made a very promising start in South Australia, why did he subsequently have such difficulty in making a living? Just what Jack Ferry meant when he wrote to the Hoches that on his return to Port Pirie Edward attempted to establish a practice, but that it was 'next to impossible then', is not clear. Was the requirement that foreign doctors pass an examination being strictly enforced by then, unlike the earlier requirement that all doctors be registered? His German medical degree was from an outstanding university, and he spoke very good English, as is obvious from his letters from Birdsville. Jack, not a man for compliments, made a point of mentioning his excellent English in one of his letters to Hamburg. Did the fact that other doctors had established themselves in Port Pirie while he was in Birdsville (Jack mentioned one, but two were called to his deathbed) mean the town was already well served? Or did Edward quite simply have a drinking problem?

A clue to his strange behaviour after Nellie's death, even perhaps to his decision to emigrate to Australia, may be found in the personality and conduct of his father, Professor Richard Hoche, who, although he responded promptly and generously to the needs of his orphan grandchildren, seems to have been an exceptionally harsh and domineering man. A history of the Johanneum school in Hamburg, of which he was headmaster from 1874 to 1888,[23] while giving him credit for being a highly educated man and an able administrator, describes him as having carried out his duties with single-minded ruthlessness. A Prussian by birth and education, he was appointed to the school when Hamburg, until 1867 an independent city, was having to adapt to life as a member of the North German Federation dominated by Prussia under Bismarck. Major changes had consequently to be made in the whole Hamburg school system and Richard Hoche was thought to be the man to implement them at the Johanneum, Hamburg's centuries-old academic school. He appears to have gone at his task with a will, in the process arousing the resentment not only of his scholars and teaching staff but of all the townspeople. 'It has been said,' the school historian writes, 'that with Richard Hoche a Prussian NCO took over the Johanneum.'[24] But it was apparently his way of dealing with people as much as his Prussian origins and his prussianisation of the school which his colleagues and pupils found galling. For instance, the history names one exceptionally gifted pupil to whom Richard Hoche's predecessor had brought 'a warm understanding', while the three years which followed under Hoche were 'a martyrdom'.[25]

When in 1888 he was appointed Superintendent of Secondary Schools in Hamburg he apparently carried his harsh regime into a wider arena, for his papers include a printed reply from Hamburg's a highest authority, the Senate, to complaints by the citizenry about the way he conducted his office.[26]

It must have been hard for Edward being the eldest son of such a stern and exacting man; harder still to have been a pupil from the age of twelve at the school of which his father was the headmaster, disliked and resented by pupils and teachers alike. But, as the German Consul's report to the Ferry family noted, he was 'kept close to his studies, the position of his father warranting such, and [had] not idled away his time'. It is not surprising, perhaps, that he had 'kicked out a little' and that it had been thought desirable that he should 'try his own way in the world', which suggests that the decision to go to Australia was not entirely his own. On the other hand, it is also possible that he himself chose to go to the furthest place he could find on the map; and when his professional career there was going badly he simply stopped writing home. Who could report failure to such a father?

Despite an apparently happy marriage and obviously close links to his wife's large family, at least up until Nellie's death, Edward in Australia seems a lonely figure. Although by the 1880s there were already a large number of Germans in South Australia, what contact he had with his fellow countrymen seems to have been limited to meeting men on visiting German ships. Although formally invited to be patron of the Port Pirie German Club, he declined, and although he himself approached the German community in Sedan about taking up practice, when told there was an opportunity there he did not avail himself of it.

5

Two Worlds : One Purpose

When Jack next wrote to the Hoches, in early February 1896, formally accepting their 'extremely kind offer' of financial help, he reported that at a Ferry family conclave it had been resolved that only half of their German grandfather's contributions should be used for the children's maintenance, the other half to be placed in the savings bank for their later education, as their early education would not be expensive. It was a generous decision, for at the time, and for many years afterwards, none of the Ferry families was more than just making ends meet and the children's grandparents were not even doing that.

The money from Germany was to arrive regularly twice a year for the next ten years, till Professor Hoche's death in 1906. On his death his two daughters, Anna and Elise, were left in considerably reduced circumstances. Writing to Jack's father-in-law, Mr Siekmann, whom she had come to know by correspondence because of his role in translating her brother Richard's letters about the maintenance money, Anna explained:

> Father's death has altogether altered our circumstances. Formerly we lived on my father's salary; later on his pension. We have now only the interest on my father's savings and what we two may earn. My sister has taken a position as nurse in a hospital for scrofulous children on the North Sea. I am trained to teach singing, elocution, theory, harmony, music history and Italian. If I am wanted here I am ready. So far I have not done much.

After further study she was to find work as a speech therapist and singing teacher and she even for a while sold life insurance to earn extra money. Her sister Lies, who was less well qualified, had to turn to and take whatever jobs were in those days available to gentlewomen, usually in charge of institutions for women or children.

Anna goes on to explain to Mr Siekmann that she and her sister had given up their father's large apartment in Hamburg because living in that city was too expensive, and that she had settled in Bad Godesberg on the Rhine, then a comparatively small town of 14 000 inhabitants. She said she had broken with the past and was now in a new place among strangers, 'independent of all old conditions'.

Middle-aged (she was forty-two), unmarried, separated from her family, and living in a town where she knew no-one, her life could have been bleak, but with her work, her music, visits to other family members, and those annual sojourns at spas which were so much a part of German middle-class life, she made the best of it. And she performed, apparently without resentment, all the duties routinely expected of maiden aunts in those days, minding Richard's children during his wife's confinements and dashing off to succour an old aunt of her own who had slipped and fallen on her head, so that, as she described it to the Ferrys, a 'hair needle' had penetrated her brain.

Yet right up to World War I Anna was to send regular cheerful and loving letters, as well as photos, postcards and presents, not just to Edward's children but to their Ferry grandmother, aunts and Uncle Jack. She asked for photos of all of them so that, as she explained, she could visualise the kind relations who were caring for the children so lovingly. Fortunately one of Nellie's cousins was a professional photographer, so from time to time studio photographs were sent.

The children wrote regularly; Uncle Jack saw to that. As soon as the financial matters had been attended to he wrote to their Uncle Richard: 'I have now instructed Frank and Edith to write to yourself and Miss Anna alternately every six months, so that you will receive your letter from Frank first in July and from Edith in January, and Miss Anna from Edith in October and Frank in March.' This was a fairly demanding regime for children who were only six and seven when they started writing. Even when they were older there was no indication in any of their letters to members of the Ferry family that they enjoyed the letters they received from Hamburg, which they rarely mention. Frank observed drily from time to time: 'I had a letter from Germany this week', and Puss at nineteen wrote: 'I received a book of German songs from Germany yesterday; I don't care for them much though.'

The children's letters to their aunts, which might have given quite another picture, have not been preserved, perhaps because they went the rounds of the Hoche relations, but the aunts' letters, in which they thank the young Hoches for letters, pictures, postage stamps, pressed flowers and, in Puss's case,

'Aunt Anna'

embroidered doilies, indicate that the children went to some trouble to please their German relatives. That Jack's original plan for them to write to their Uncle Richard and Aunt Anna was adhered to seems doubtful, since none of the letters has survived. Their German grandfather reportedly followed all their activities with great interest but his deteriorating eyesight made it impossible for him either to read or to write letters.

Anna never ceased to hope that the children would one day pay their Hamburg relatives a visit. In 1897, for instance, she wrote to their aunt Edith Inglis: 'Perhaps when [the children] are grown up they may come here to visit us, or to choose a profession here, or to marry here or to do anything else here. Now you will laugh at me, that does my father always when I am laying out plans for the orphans.' And when Puss became engaged Anna hoped that when she married she and her husband would 'make a long and wide wedding excursion to Germany'.

Anna Hoche wrote of music, the beauties of the Rhine, and the 'dear Kaiser' and his family. She waxed ecstatic in 1904 about preparations for a one-day visit to Hamburg by Britain's King Edward VII, and concluded sympathetically:

> In the evening he will return very fatigued to Kiel, where he is stationed as a guest of our Emperor for all the sail regattas . . . To these regattas all possible princes and Lords come together. It is a splendid circle that moves at the shore of the sea.

Anna also sent the children sheet music and books in English specially ordered from London, and begged them to name any music or books they would like her to send them. She obviously imagined their early exposure to music to be on a more elevated plane than is betrayed by one inspector's report on the singing in the Napperby school in their grandfather, John Ferry's, time as headmaster: 'Singing: Girls good. Boys don't open their teeth.' [27] She followed everything they did with the greatest interest. When Frank mentioned winning a scholarship to the Adelaide School of Mines, she wrote back:

We can not understand quite rightly what means School of Mines and I cannot find a fitting expression in the dictionary. Please explain it once. When you are visiting this school you must be still in a scientific school, am I right? When you are in the School of Mines are you then at Port Pirie or somewhere else? And what subjects do you study in that school and how old must you be to go there and are you able to make an official examination when leaving that school? Your aunt Anna is a very curious one but grandfather, too, likes to understand very much about his grandchildren.

A printed prospectus of the School, sent shortly afterwards by the children's grandmother, Emma, only served to increase her puzzlement: 'I have read it but I did not understand everything in it. Very astonished was I that "tailer science" is instructed there, too.' The prospectus was now being studied 'very attentively' by her brothers as well. Her puzzlement is understandable, for to have her nephew starting at the age of fifteen the kind of studies which, in Germany, he would have started only at nineteen or twenty was very strange. When later he sent her his exam papers, and eventually his diploma, she pronounced them 'quite other' from such documents in Germany.

She was less at sea when writing to Puss about her musical studies, reassured by letters and concert programmes which showed her niece was playing the works of the great European composers.

While there can be no doubting the warmth of the German aunts' long-distance affection for the children, their letters suggest that the Hoche family also cherished high expectations for their future. Sure of its position in the Hamburg establishment, the family had for many generations educated its sons to take their place in the learned professions, its daughters to take theirs in cultured society. Things were solid: salaries and pensions were paid in good time, dwellings were comfortable, servants available; family members could expect to live out their lives as their parents had and when they died their furniture and possessions would pass to the younger generation, just as they always had. What more natural than for them to think that their money was being used to ensure that Edward's children were educated to follow in the family tradition? The closeness with which not only Anna but the entire Hoche family followed Frank's school and School of Mines performance and Puss's musical studies betrays the family's expectations that somehow, despite all, Edward's children would end up in the family mould.

Anna also gave family news: 'My sister has been till the beginning of October at a small bath [spa] on the North Sea but she has frozen from the first till the last day during night and day.' What a picture that must have conjured up in the minds of the children! And what would they have made of her report of the prowess of her one-year-old niece, her brother Richard's Ady? 'She can stand lonely now but not yet go.' (She can stand alone but not yet walk.) Another time (in 1913) she told Frank, now a young man, that she would make him a copy of what she called their pedigree. We have it still. With German thoroughness and exactitude her brother Richard had traced the Hoche family back through generations of professional people to a simple peasant family living near the Harz Mountains in 1603. Their name is said to derive from the high (in German *hoch*) position of their cottage.

The children's other German aunt, Elise or Lies, only wrote very occasionally, perhaps because of her demanding jobs in institutions; doubtless also because she was ill frequently and for long periods. Both sisters suffered badly from asthma. Elise clearly found writing English more difficult than Anna did, though Anna also usually had a dictionary at her side, as her choice of words betrays. Elise's letters lacked the enthusiasm and warmth of her sister's, though she was obviously at pains to write about things she thought might interest the children. She gave fascinating little insights into life in Hamburg. On one occasion she told the children that their Uncle Ludwig (the doctor) had come to the city on 'a very serious occupation with several other gentlemen'. She explained:

> They had to inspect the ships' arrangements against the pest [plague] and naturally they must surprise every captain, that he could not make last [minute] preparations. And therefore these gentlemen were forced to go on the water at 6 o'clock, when darkness was everywhere. It was a very disagreeable message they had to fulfil but they saw interesting things . . . The pest did not come here, only some rats died by it in their dark space under the warehouses . . . Hamburg is built near the harbour so narrow and dirty, that every illness [such] as cholera and pest and others always becomes very bad in those districts.

On another occasion, in 1897, she described to them the consecration ceremony of Hamburg's new town hall. The old one had been burnt down, she told them, in 1842, when nearly half of the city was destroyed. She was full of praise for the new edifice: 'One room is quite sculptured in wood by the little orphans, all windows, doors, walls and ceilings. Three hundred children have carved for a year.' Puss would have been eight and Frank seven when they received this letter; there is no record of their reaction to this account of the gargantuan labours of those other orphans.

When Jack Ferry wrote he explained droughts and the high price of feed, and gave summer temperatures of 110°F and higher. From time to time he mentioned salaries of family members, his own as station master at Caltowie as £190 and (much later) £250 per annum, his sister Edith's husband's as £230, as post-master at Balaklava, and these give us an idea of the value of the £50 a year the children were receiving from Hamburg. He also had plenty to say about events on the other side of the world. He disapproved of Britain's support of the Turks against the Russians: 'Colonials do not admire the Turks, nor their ways, except that they are good fighters. Personally I think Eastern Christians would be better under Russia.' He sympathised with what he called Germany's 'tight' position in Europe but added:

> Militarism does not, happily, oppress us as it does you. Our
> time is therefore devoted to social necessities. It will indeed be
> a blessing to civilisation when the nations of Europe agree to
> dispense with their huge military burdens . . . An armed peace
> is a dreadful strain on nations.

Anna, too, had moments of tactlessness, though rarely. Writing to
the children's grandmother, Emma, in 1901, she said she hoped
Emma had good news of her son Roland, who was fighting in
the Boer War. 'It is a pity', she wrote, 'what a number of young
lives are sacrificed there and for what purpose? Only that a few
members of the English nation may get more and more
money. . . But it is better I write not about that—our opinion is
probably not the same, you are an English woman and we are
German people.' However, the warm penfriendship which grew
up between the two women seems not to have suffered as a
result of these rare lapses.

What the families in this correspondence, particularly the
children, made of the letters and photos they received, and how
they envisaged each others' lifestyles, can only be guessed
at. There seem, perhaps predictably, to have been big gaps in
the Hamburg family's understanding of what life was like in far-
off South Australia. The Ferry family, whose older members
had grown up in their father's boarding school near London and
knew London well, and who maintained a keen interest in events
in Europe, had probably a fair idea of how a middle-class family
would live in a European city. Emma, too, had grown up in
London. The studio photographs they sent to Hamburg show
that when the occasion demanded they could dress for the middle
class European way of life. When the Hoches asked for photos
of the children after Nellie died, Ferry sewing and lacemaking
skills turned Pussie and Frank out in velvet and lace before they
were taken to the studio to be photographed. And a studio group
photograph sent to Hamburg many years later shows Emma and

six of her daughters beautifully gowned. (Nellie had died by this time.) By then all but one of the daughters had married, so money would have been easier to come by. Perhaps the studio photos which were sent helped to foster the Hoches' illusions about life down under, and even in the few casual snapshots found among the Ferry papers Emma is always pictured wearing a gown to the ground, with a white lace collar or fichu and little white lace bonnet. We know that at least some casual snapshots were sent to Germany, for in 1897 her aunt Lies wrote to Puss that they had been thrilled to receive from one of the children's Australian aunts photos of their grandparents, aunts and uncles and their 'houses and places', but the only casual photo that has survived among the German papers is one of Puss and Frank, aged about six and five, romping happily with their three youngest aunts, who are dressed in long dresses and straw boaters. Doubtless the snapshots, like the children's letters, were circulated among the various Hoche households and never came back to Anna to be preserved.

The photographs the Ferrys received of the Hoche house in Hamburg showed it to be large and handsomely furnished with solid antiques, gossamer-fine lace curtains and a profusion of indoor plants. The house went with Professor Hoche's last job as Superintendent of Secondary Schools in Hamburg, and even when he retired and they had to move, their new home, as Anna described it, was a spacious ground floor apartment with a garden, opposite the Zoological Gardens (Verbindungsbahn 8), where concerts were held almost every afternoon. She complained of a high turnover of servants: 'In a large town it is very difficult to keep good servants . . . They prefer to go to the factory where they are without control during the night and may dance and do other foolish things.' When Richard Hoche's wife and two little daughters arrived to stay with his family in Hamburg they brought one of their own maids with them.

But it would be surprising if any photos were sent to Hamburg of the 'apartment' in which Emma and John Ferry were living at this stage in Napperby, near Port Pirie, John's last teaching post,

Emma Ferry and six of her seven daughters. *Left to right:* Mabel,
Emma, Mary-Louisa, Emma Ferry, Florena, Isabella and Edith.

where he was headteacher from 1884 to 1891. The school was
housed in a building which had been the dining room of the
shearers' quarters at the Napperby outstation, and the teacher's
family lived in 'additional small rooms attached to the classroom
[which] . . . had been used by the shearer's cook'. An inspector's
report on the premises noted: 'white ants are continually
running off with the woodwork.'[28]

Though the children dutifully wrote to their German relatives
about their progress at school, they seem to have written nothing
about their physical surroundings in the Napperby primary school
in which they spent their first few school years, probably
because to them these were unremarkable. To the Hamburg
Hoches they would have been unimaginable. School records
and the reports of various school inspectors enable us to picture
them. The schoolroom and headmaster's ramshackle dwelling
were in a paddock, where one would expect to find shearers'
quarters, and adjacent to them was a large dam, where the
children who rode or drove to school would water their horses
at lunchtime. The horses 'were not allowed to run loose in the

playground or be tied to the school fence, but [had to be] left in a fenced-off part of the yard'. The dam had been built at the edge of a track, over which stock from as far north as Marree made its way south. Cattle and sheep in their thousands stopped to water at the dam. Occasionally a camel train with its Afghan cameleers would call in for a drink and a rest, and with luck the children would be treated to bone-jolting camel rides.[29]

Though much damaged by white ants, the schoolroom was roomy enough, a rectangle some twenty-five feet long and fifteen feet wide. 'Half way along the eastern wall stood an iron stove . . . the only means of heating the room, and on rainy days there was an array of shoes and garments drying out for use at going home time.' On a lean-to porch of galvanised iron the school's washing facilities were placed—'two white enamelled bowls . . . one at each end . . . for boys and girls'. Apparently there were two toilets also, doubtless of the wooden-seated, hole-in-the-ground kind, as one inspector reported: 'The seat of the boys' WC needs an immediate scrubbing.'[30] (This was after John Ferry's time.)

The drinking facilities consisted of 'a tubular-shaped water bag suspended from the shed roof . . . with a tin pannikin attached to it by a piece of string'. 'It was used by all the children,' the town's history tells us, 'and as the only outbreak of disease of any magnitude was head lice, they must have been a hardy lot.'[31] Nor was the sharing of the pannikin the school's only health hazard. A note among the school archives records: 'A boy saw a snake creep into our wood heap. Mrs Bain kindly came to our help and shot it.'[32]

But in far-off Hamburg the Hoches knew nothing of such things. They seem to have had no idea, even after reading the regular letters from the Ferrys, of the rawness and toughness of life in the colony, particularly in the newly-settled country districts of north-central South Australia where Ferry family members mostly lived. On the contrary, their letters indicate that they saw South Australia as a transplanted corner of

Europe. Thus, when Puss, having finished her musical studies in Adelaide, told Anna how sorry she was to be returning to Port Pirie and how she would miss the concerts and other musical opportunities of Adelaide, her aunt wrote to console her: 'As for your returning to Port Pirie, it is not so bad to be at a small place. Bad Godesberg is really not a large one but I find so much interest for all branches of music.' She went on to suggest that Puss might consider holding musical soirées in Port Pirie, carefully explaining what a soirée was, and adding encouragingly that the initiative of one person might really succeed in changing a place. In Bad Godesberg Anna was living across the street from the railway station and could be in Bonn in nine minutes. Port Pirie, a bustling port for grain and metals built on mudflats, had by that time some 8000 residents and resembled the charming old Rhine town, with all its cultural opportunities, in only one respect: they were both near the water.

Even in the sisters' reduced circumstances after their father's death, they could write of frequent concerts and occasional pleasure travel—to the Tyrol, Salzburg, the Vosges Mountains,

Napperby: probable site of John Ferry's house

Berlin, Dresden, and the Harz Mountains—and of their brother Ludwig's plans to take his wife to North America, or for an extended stay in Italy. Anna wrote with pride that the train journey between Hamburg and Berlin took only four hours, and that there were plans for a service taking only one and a quarter hours. What did she make of Jack's matter-of-fact report in one of his letters that in his new posting to the little copper town of Moonta, where he was harbour master, he was also in charge of the horse-drawn railway?

Only very rarely does one sense a sudden insight on Anna's part, as when, more than two years after Nellie's death, she replies to a letter from Nellie's sister Edith: 'We did not know that Nelly died so far from her family, alone with husband and children in distressed circumstances.' Or when she asks Puss: 'Write me how far is the way from Port Pirie to Napperby and in what manner you must ['go', crossed out] walk from one place to another. [The German word *gehen* means both 'to go' and 'to walk'.] And how long is the way?' The 'way' was about eleven kilometres on a country track, along which family members either walked or rode in their horse-drawn cart.

The Hoche family also seems not to have realised that, while the various members of the Ferry family made considerable sacrifices in order to ensure that Nellie's and Edward's children had the kind of education which would help them to make their way in the world, they were not able to give their own children similar advantages. Only one of the Hoche children's many Australian cousins, Jack's eldest son, received a tertiary education (he joined Frank at the School of Mines). The girls were expected to marry, the boys to take what work they could find, on the land, in the railways or in the postal service, just as their fathers had.

Jack's letters certainly never mentioned such matters, though he regularly kept Hamburg up with the children's whereabouts, as they moved from one relative to another, depending on where their schooling required them to be at any given time and who could conveniently have them to stay.

Edith is at present staying with her Aunt Edith at Balaklava . . . Little Leonard is at present with my sister Bella, Mrs Stewart, at Port Pirie. I am pleased that he can be there for a while as he will have frequent opportunities to spend time with Frank and also Edith, when she returns. We wish them to grow up as familiar to each other as possible so that they will learn to feel towards each other as brothers and sisters should.

Jack need not have had any worries on that score. When Puss and Frank, as young adults, were boarding in Adelaide, their boarding house keeper commented to someone on how devoted they were to each other, and how they never quarrelled, unlike another brother and sister boarding in her establishment. On being told of this, their grandmother, Emma, wrote to Jack's wife, Lena: 'Pussie and Frank never did quarrel and we have long ago found out that if we offended one we offended the other.'

Though there was never over many years any indication in the Ferry correspondence that the children were anything but welcome in their various households, they seem to have been acutely aware of the precariousness of their situation and of their obligations to the relatives with whom they stayed. Frank writes to Uncle Jack that Aunt Bella is having him to stay and taking no board:

> I give as little trouble as possible and do all in my power to help about the garden, wood heap, etc. I get all my washing and ironing done out, have dinner every day at school and tea in town about twice a week.

Apparently his efforts to be as little trouble as possible to this aunt paid off, for a month later he writes to his grandmother:

> Auntie Bell and I seem to agree much better than we used to. Perhaps it is because I know her better, and realise the importance of keeping my temper under trying circumstances. Such circumstances are rare certainly, but none the less trying for all that. Auntie Bell is very good to me and I fear I have not treated her with as much consideration as I might. But lately I have just begun to see many things in a different light to what I used to.

He is nineteen by now, and obviously looking seriously at the implications of his dependent situation, perhaps with an occasional reminder from Uncle Jack, for a few days later he assures Uncle Jack: 'Puss and I fully realise Grandmother's great goodness to us . . . It is only of late years that we have understood what she in particular, but others also, have done for us. I shall be very glad when I can get permanent work.'

Despite the added burden of having an extra child or children added to their own, the Ferry relatives seem to have had extraordinary goodwill towards the young Hoches. When Frank and Puss were studying and boarding in Adelaide, aunts and uncles visiting Adelaide seem always to have looked them up and provided treats: meals out or a night at the opera. If Frank felt that he was a bit old at sixteen to enjoy the panto-mime of Cinderella, there was no hint of this when he wrote appreciatively to Uncle Jack of the 'treat' a visiting aunt and uncle had given Puss and him. And he seems to have been eager to play his part in the implicit bargain with his relatives, as when he went to the Adelaide railway station to meet an aunt passing through, and looked after her till it was time to take her back to the station on the following day.

Nor were the children's Ferry relations the only people from whom they received great help and kindness. To Jack's wife, Lena, in 1906 Emma wrote appreciatively of what Lena's family, the Siekmanns, had done for the children: 'I am sure your brothers and father have been most kind and attentive to both of them. They have told us of their visits and drives to Norwood. Indeed they have never experienced anything other than kindness from every-one.' Mr Siekmann had been a tower of strength to the family ever since he had asked the Consul to make inquiries in Hamburg about Edward; he and Anna Hoche corresponded regularly, once she learned of his role in translating Richard's letters, and when he was eighty she was still sending him birthday greetings.

Friends were not the only people outside the family to be concerned for the Hoche children's welfare. Their teachers, wherever they were studying, aware probably of their need to succeed, seem to have given them extra help on many occasions. And one of their boarding house keepers in Adelaide was apparently equally solicitous for their wellbeing. In 1908 Puss, now nineteen, was boarding with a Mrs Jacoby, while Frank was apparently boarding elsewhere. Puss wrote to Jack: 'Mrs Jacoby is concerned over Frank's looks and says he is not fed properly, so she has asked him to come to live here until his year's up. I don't know if he's coming, but hope he is, as he does look wretched.' (Mrs Jacoby had a rather special link with the children. Her husband had been at school in Hamburg with two Hoche boys. Asked, in a letter from Puss, whether these could have been her brothers, Anna replied that they must have been, for there were no other Hoches at the school.)

Though Jack doled out the money from Germany, Grandmother Emma was the one who took responsibility for the well-being of the children and the one to whom they turned when there was some doubt about their living arrangements. So it was to her that Frank wrote when, aged seventeen and boarding in Adelaide, he learnt from a cousin that the aunt with whom he was to spend the holidays was ill. 'That means I cannot stay at their place for the holidays, and also that she will not be able to fix up my socks, handkerchiefs, underpants etc. I wish you would write and tell me what to do about the holidays.' It was Emma who organised which of their aunts would make the children's clothes, sometimes turning to and making them herself. When little Len was still living with Jack and Lena, Emma wrote to Lena:

> Am sending a parcel for Lenny, two shirts and two pairs of underpants, as those he took are only fit to wear during warm weather. Don't look at the sewing, as I have made them by hand. [Her sewing machine was on loan to one of her daughters.] I have also made two new flannels, one shirt and two pairs of underpants for Frank to take back with him. This next week Puss goes up to Mabel's for Floss [the children's youngest and only unmarried aunt] to alter her last winter's dress as it is

rather tight for her in the armholes. She will only require another blouse, so their sewing will soon be done.

While Emma expected her daughters to have the children to live with them when their education required them to be away from Port Pirie, and to help her with their sewing (as she from time to time helped them with theirs), she herself was prepared to see to most of the tasks parents expect to undertake for their children. (Jack lived at some distance from Port Pirie so only saw them on his annual vacation.) 'I obtained the students' travelling forms,' she writes to Jack, 'and sent them to the children so that they could be filled out before they leave.' And, some years later, 'I'm wondering how you manage about paying Miss Jervis [with whom Puss and Frank were then boarding in Adelaide] during holidays, whether the same, or whether half, or if you pay at all. The state school teachers do not pay but Malcolm [her daughter Mabel's husband] says it is the custom in Melbourne and Sydney only to pay half.'

When she wrote this Emma was in her seventies, and she had, after all, raised fourteen children of her own. And even for an era when large families were common, and living conditions for country families fairly primitive, her married life had been exceptionally difficult. Not just because her family was large and money always short, but because the family had had to move house so often. In all they moved to seven different country schools. For a period John tried, with disastrous results, to make a better living farming, and this entailed three more moves. On the farms the housing was even worse than that provided with the schools or, in one instance, non-existent. On the first block, in Gladstone, there was only a two-roomed hut to house the (by then) thirteen of them, and a brackish well—not even a tank for rainwater. John had made a large tent for the move and added a lean-to room and a brick oven to the hut. The girls slept in the tent and the boys under a canvas contraption rigged up on two hoops over the waggon while John and his older sons worked on the addition to the hut. On the next block, in the Hundred

of Pirie, there was no house and no provision at all for water, so
Emma and the younger children were left behind in Gladstone
while John and his two eldest sons built a five-roomed house,
with a kitchen of galvanised iron with a brick oven and brick
floor. Only then did they fetch Emma and the younger children
and furniture in the bullock wagon, spring cart and dray. Though
a rainwater tank was installed and dams were dug, water remained
a problem and at times it had to be carted from a well five miles
away, even for the stock. The water shortage usually also frequently
doomed attempts to grow fruit and vegetables to help feed the
family, a family which during this farming phase grew by three.
When eventually John returned to teaching he moved, after a
brief period at the school at Terowie, to Napperby, where, as we
have seen, the family lived in the 'additional small
rooms . . . which had been used by the shearers' cook'. Yet John
wrote to his father from there saying the accommodation was
much better than what they had had hitherto.

6

Going for 100 Per Cent

Emma had earned a restful and secure old age, and this she was eventually to enjoy, for she lived to be ninety-five, but in her seventies her principal concern was for the Hoche children. She followed their progress closely and rejoiced in their successes. Edith and Frank were exceptionally good scholars, who aimed at marks of 100 per cent and frequently got them. Less is known about Len, though the Hamburg relatives expressed pleasure that he was such a good scholar, and an excellent report provided by his headmaster proved decisive in his getting his first job.

On finishing at high school, Edith went on to study pianoforte at the Elder Conservatorium of Music in Adelaide. Frank, who attended the Port Pirie School of Mines for his secondary schooling, won the Adelaide School of Mines country scholarship in 1906. This gave him free tuition in any subject and a living allowance of £30 a year for three years. Emma followed his progress approvingly: at the end of first term, she told Jack, he had got 100 per cent for euclid and mensuration, and 87 per cent for algebra; the other results were not yet out. The following term it was 100 per cent for two subjects, with no subject under 85 per cent. When his scholarship ran out in 1909 he was given a second scholarship of the same amount, which saw him through to the end of his course.

Little is known of Len's achievements, except that he did well at school, because for most of his childhood he lived either with his grandmother or with his Uncle Jack, so that his needs were met on the spot and involved little correspondence. Surprisingly, Jack seems not to have insisted that he write to his German relatives. Anna mentioned just one or two letters from him and surmised, on one occasion, that he did not like to write to his old German aunts, but she always inquired about him and included him in her gifts and greetings. This is not to say, however, that Len's interests were neglected. On the contrary, both his grandmother and his Uncle Jack gave much thought to his education and future prospects. Answering a letter from Jack in 1908, when Len would have been fifteen, Emma writes:

> Yes, he seems to have no idea whatever of what he will do in the future. The only thing he has said is that he would like to take chemistry and physics at the local [i.e. Port Pirie] School of Mines, but some time since I asked him if he would not like to get into a bank. Yes, he thought that would be alright, so I at once told him he must take more pains with his writing. I met Mr Tuck, the new headmaster; he told me that he was much pleased with him. He was bright and intelligent and had a very pleasing manner, which, of course, I knew all about! [And in another letter to Jack] I don't think he is as enthusiastic as Frank, but then he is not so old.

Jack was particularly fond of Len, who had lived with him and Lena from when he was brought back as a baby from Birdsville till at the age of three he went to his grandparents in Napperby because Lena was expecting a fourth child. In one of his letters to Germany Jack refers to him as 'our little boy' and writes with a parent's pride in his progress.

Both Edith and Frank had to live in Adelaide to continue their studies, and since for the first time the Ferry network could provide no obliging relative for them to live with, it was the Hamburg money, most of which had been saved, that made this possible. Realising that a small amount of money had to go a long way, Jack kept a tight rein, disbursing it only in response to detailed claims in writing from Frank, who usually put in for

Frank Hoche as a student

Edith's needs as well. Weekly board, haircuts, boot blacking, epsom salts, the cost of having a tooth drawn, everything had to be itemised. When they moved from place to place they had to ask for two or three shillings to have their heavy boxes carried because, as Frank reminded Uncle Jack, they had no portmanteau. Usually by the time Frank wrote they were down to two or three shillings. On one occasion he was obliged to borrow two shillings and sixpence from Mr Siekmann to buy drawing paper so he could complete an assignment on time.

Jack was sometimes late in sending the money for board and Frank always dreaded having to remind him. 'Dear Uncle Jack, I hope you won't think me rude but you seem to have forgotten that our board was due on the 20th,' he wrote on the 28th of the month. Jack, of course, was bringing up his own four children and looking after his busy railway stations at Caltowie and, later, Balaklava. He was also constantly striving to earn a little extra money by various means, such as raising cattle, as well as being

Len Hoche as a boy

actively involved in community affairs, especially cricket, his great love. That he occasionally forgot the Hoche children's deadlines is hardly surprising.

Edith's main educational expenses were her Conservatorium fees of five guineas a term, her board, and payment for the use of the piano at her boarding house, but Frank's share trickled out in endless small payments for such things as tools, India ink and blueprints for his engineering. He economised whenever he could, buying equipment second-hand or jointly with another student, and selling each year's books at year's end. He had put his scholarship money into Jack's care, as he did one guinea he won at a shooting match, for he was an excellent shot. (In later years he was to be the claybird shooting champion of Victoria.) But he still felt the need to apologise for asking Jack for money, concluding one letter with: 'I'm sorry I am so expensive.' In another letter to Jack, when he was sixteen, he describes a gruelling session at the dentist, who had failed to extract all the pieces of an impacted and infected tooth, making a return visit necessary, and concludes anxiously: 'Don't think he'll charge any more.'

He usually waited till his clothes were threadbare before asking for money to replace them. 'My everyday suit has got so shabby I think I will have to get another at once as it is coming out at the elbows. I do not like asking because my clothing was such an expensive item last term but I've kept it going as long as I can. Am also in need of a pair of boots.' A month later he wrote again, more urgently: 'I say, I wish you'd hurry up and write about my suit please, because I'm really in none too good a state (except on Sunday when I'm a "toff").' He denied himself most outings because of the expense. His Uncle Alfred Pearce had given him a rifle, but on at least one occasion he missed the chance of a shooting trip because of the cost and because it would mean taking time off from study. He told Jack he would be passing up the School of Mines ball as he couldn't dance and it would have been too expensive to get shoes and gloves, adding: 'I do not think I would enjoy it much except perhaps the supper.' Happily the dancing lessons he could not afford were eventually provided without payment by the sister of one of his uncles by marriage who had a dancing school, and then he reported to Jack that his social life had taken off.

Frank had wanted to do medicine, but needed to win a scholarship and be able to earn money during his course, so he settled for mining and metallurgy because there would be more opportunities to get holiday jobs. When at the Adelaide School of Mines he was always on the lookout for holiday work. Though none of his uncles lived near enough to be helpful in finding it, his uncles by marriage were a great help: a word to a friend in the Port Pirie smelters, or a plea to the Broken Hill mine manager usually brought an offer of work. Uncle Jack was reluctant to let him work underground at Broken Hill when he was seventeen, but Frank pleaded:

Those that went last year are all going again. None of them found the work too hard, except that at first the closeness underground made them feel funny for a day or two . . . Professor Chapman says a fellow should not sit for the final unless he has seen some experience in a mine . . . Think it over will you, and tell me how you like it.

In the summer holidays of 1907, when he was seventeen, work was particularly hard to get. Emma wrote to Jack: 'You will not be surprised to learn that Frank is getting tired of looking for tallying work; he said he would try to get on at the smelters, as he would be sure to get a wrinkle that would help him in his metallurgy course, besides earning some money for himself.' Thanks to a word from an uncle, Frank had got work at the BHP mine, working on a night shift from midnight till 8 a.m. Emma went on:

This went on for a week, but as usual he met with an accident and some molten lead got on his foot. He made very light of it. Mabel dressed it, and he still went on with his work. Malcolm became uneasy when it would not heal, so he spoke to the mine manager, who said he must cease work at once, as the lead contained poison, so poor Frank had to give in, but he earned £4.10.0. Then Frank heard of poll clerks being wanted, so Clem [a cousin] got him a position there from yesterday, for which he will receive a guinea, but only fancy, just the day before [he was to start] he was going to Solomon Town on a borrowed bike when just in front of the wine saloon a whelping little cur ran in front of his wheel. The bike capsized, threw Frank, and he had nasty wounds on his elbow and knee, besides tearing his pants. However, he was at his place at the poll yesterday. He will be leaving for school on Monday. I think he is the right kind of boy.

Edith had few opportunities to work; nor would it have been expected of her. During her vacations she practised her piano for eight hours a day, and it was doubtless then that she acquired from her aunts the domestic skills and dazzling 'accomplishments' she was to demonstrate in later years. In her final year she reluctantly took payment for teaching music to a young cousin in order to be able to afford extra coaching in music theory for herself.

Her hopes of working towards the AMUA (Associate in Music from the University of Adelaide) looked very remote, for by the time she had completed her first two years at the Conservatorium her German grandfather had died and the Hoche funds were very low. Jack, conscious of the fact that the two older children had had more of the Hamburg money than Len, was anxious to keep what little was left for him. Emma wrote to the Director of the Conservatorium, explaining that Edith was an orphan, and that now that her German grandfather had died no money could be found for her to continue her course; on her splendid results and strong recommendations from her teachers, Puss was awarded a free place for her final year.

But the problem of paying for her board in Adelaide remained. Emma had been hoping that she could board with her Aunt Bella, who by then was living in Adelaide, but Bella apparently was unable to have her. What is more, Bella had not replied to Emma's letter asking her to have Puss; the unwelcome news had come on the family grapevine. The unheard-of had happened—even Puss was surprised when her grandmother told her—and Emma was reported as being very upset. Only later did she learn from Frank that Bella had been ill.

Emma at this time was living in Port Pirie with her second daughter, Louisa, and her husband Arthur Ewens, and it was to Arthur she turned for advice. It was with him and his wife that Puss had spent most of her childhood, for they had four daughters around her age. Emma wrote to Jack that Arthur was very anxious Puss should take up the scholarship and had advertised in two Adelaide dailies for board for her. He had had several replies and was inclined to accept the offer of a Mrs Jacoby, on whom Adelaide friends had given him a favourable report. Was there enough Hoche money left to pay even part of the board?

The new term started in two weeks' time.

Four days later Arthur also wrote to Jack;

> I may tell you—perhaps you already know—that she is growing
> into a splendid woman and already possesses heaps of accom-
> plishments in addition to her most brilliant pianoforte playing.
> I really predict for her a future that will do credit to us all and
> herself in particular. For, as confirmed by the certificates she
> holds, I have never so much admired [any]one's industry and
> smartness. This schooling is her life and soul, and like her fine
> young brothers, Frank and Len, there is nothing any trouble to
> her, and their prosperity is assured with what assistance we can
> give them now.

He went on to say that Puss and Frank had promised to make
full provision for the return of Len's share of the Hoche money
once they were earning, adding: 'It is a pleasure to help these
good children.'

Anna Hoche's letters make it clear that she knew it was likely
that lack of money would prevent Puss from completing her
course, but there was a presumption in them that there was
some elasticity in Ferry money resources. She wrote to say she
was sorry she was not able to help but perhaps their grandmother
could find the money. Of course, she would have been well
aware of the considerable help her father had given the children,
but there was never any suggestion that her brothers, by then
well-established in their professions, might possibly have helped
out in this crisis.

In the end Jack made available the money needed, albeit
reluctantly, and till the end of his days seems to have worried
that Len had not had his fair share. At the age of ninety-two he
sent Frank the little second-hand savings bank book (it had
belonged to an order of nuns till the bank failed, as he carefully
noted in the book) in which, over a period of ten years, he had
recorded the Hoche money going in and out. In all, he had
disbursed £614 15s 1d, which sum included Frank's scholarship

money. He wrote: 'You will notice that the balance of funds shown . . . is £17 8s 7d, all the residue after Edith and yourself had finished your respective periods of education, so that your brother Leonard did not enjoy the educational advantages of you two elder ones.' He went on to say that after giving Len a chance to follow 'pastoral pursuits', at which he was not successful, he had made the money up to £30 out of his own funds and given it to him, and he reminded Frank that the latter had then found work for Len with BHP. Though Len, by his own wish, never underwent any training after he left school, Frank and Puss were to give him financial and other help from time to time throughout his life. He, like Frank, had had a secret wish to study medicine, but knew that the money could never be found to put him through such a long and expensive course.

The little bank book also shows that Jack, like the others of Nellie's siblings who had helped to bring up the children, had not taken a penny of the Hamburg money. Jack confirmed this in his last letter to Frank. Only their grandmother, who during her husband's last illness and her long widowhood had very little income, had received small amounts to cover some of what she spent on the children.

Puss had her extra year and in 1908, when she was nineteen, got her AMUA. The Conservatorium staff had done everything they could in her final year to help her, and towards the end of the year she wrote to Jack:

> Dr Ennis was talking to me for a while in his room today and as usual he asked me if I could stay longer than this year. I convinced him on that point and said I hoped to be teaching next year. And what do you think he is going to do? Give me lessons about twice a month on 'How to Teach!' Isn't that grand, and very good of him, don't you think?

One year later Frank, too, completed his formal studies at the Adelaide School of Mines in conjunction with Adelaide University. He obtained his Diploma in Metallurgy in 1911 and in Mining in 1917, after fulfilling the necessary conditions of practical experience in each case. In 1910 he had gone to work for BHP, and was to remain with the company till his retirement, rising to a top management position as General Superintendent of Mines and Quarries. Mindful, no doubt, of his own youth, he was always very concerned to give young men opportunities for advancement, and when in 1950 he was awarded the Bronze Medal of the Australasian Institute of Mining and Metallurgy particular mention was made of 'his splendid work in the training of young men for Australian industry'.

In 1910, ten months after finishing her studies, Puss stunned her grandmother by accepting a proposal of marriage from Alfred Howard, a man twice her age. Emma seems to have been the only one in the family who was surprised, as she told Jack:

> I must own that I was nearly off my head when I first heard of the unexpected proposal and still more of the acceptance of same, although Arthur says he has seen it coming a long while. I don't think I met Howard more than 5 or 6 times before. Although the girls here have laughed at Howard's attentions I never took the thing seriously on account of the disparity in age, but on looking back I can see that for over 12 months he has walked home with Puss from teaching etc., but as he has always been interested in both Frank and Puss I never gave it a second thought . . . I wish Mr Howard, as you say, was only 10 years younger, but he is a keen business man of unblemished character, kind and thoughtful and, above everything else, a most temperate man. Arthur thinks that Puss will have a good home and Howard's first care will be her happiness. Moreover, according to Arthur, he must be getting £500 per annum from Barrier Wharf Co.; his mother, who was a Miss Cave, sometime before her death sold out her interest in Cave and Co., but with what results I am not able to say—it is only just lately that these matters have interested me.

Emma's money concerns were of a quite different order. She had been a widow for seven years, and was receiving a small pension 'collected for her from the post-office', which suggests a government pension. She was seventy-three, so would have been eligible for the age pension under the *Invalid and Old-age Pensions Act* of 1908. As it was paid at a maximum of £52 a year, and was severely means-tested not only on any other income but on the pensioner's home, she certainly would not have had to contemplate large sums of money. She and her youngest daughter, Flossie, even moved out of the tiny Port Pirie house they were living in after John Ferry's death and from then on lived with one or other of Emma's daughters.

As Arthur predicted, Puss did have a good home, and plenty of help in the house to help her care for the eight children born to her in the next few years. But in 1927, when Alfred was sixty and Puss only thirty-eight, he died suddenly, leaving her and the children, whose ages ranged from thirteen to three, very little to live on. However, her musical and other talents and the tenacity so evident in her younger days, plus considerable help from Frank, enabled her to provide for her family until the older children had had some training and entered the workforce.

Frank married Kathleen Isabel Butler in 1918. Before his marriage, and at the request of his future father-in-law, he changed his name to Hockey, which was how it had always been pronounced in his growing-up years. He did not do so unwillingly, for by the end of the war he had become very anti-German and was to remain so for the rest of his life. No doubt what he had been told about the circumstances of his father's death were an element in this; and the war had hit the Ferry family hard. Though he himself had not been allowed to enlist, being in a reserved occupation, Len and a number of their cousins had. Len had been wounded at Gallipoli and gassed on the Western Front, and returned home suffering from 'shell shock', while his eldest aunt and her husband, Emma and

Alfred Pearce, had lost all their three sons on the Western Front, one of them killed at Len's side. So it is perhaps not surprising that Frank made no attempt when the war was over to trace his German relatives. Though he was briefly in Germany on business in 1921, he did not try to discover their whereabouts. Len, incidentally, retained the original spelling of the name, and seems to have been, at least in later life, quite proud of his German origins. He married Merla Enid Cowled in 1921.

Edith "Pussie" Hoche at the time of her marriage

7

The German Connection Again

Like his forebears on both sides, Frank valued education highly
and made sure his three daughters had a good one. Though
he firmly believed that a woman's place was in the home, and
rather reluctantly agreed to tertiary studies, his sister Edith's
experience persuaded him that all women should be equipped
to earn their own living if need be. He even agreed to his youngest
daughter, Athel, doing medicine, though he pronounced it 'no
career for a woman'.

His other two daughters, myself and my sister Barbara, both
in our late teens, spent 1938 in Europe studying languages. While
doing a short summer course for teachers of German abroad at
Munich University, we started to search for our father's aunts.
We had seen a copy of the Hoche family tree, the 'pedigree'
Anna had sent the children, but we had no idea of the aunts'
whereabouts, nor even if they were still alive.

On a visit to Stuttgart, we made enquiries at an Institute for
Germans Abroad and were given the address of a German writer
called Alfred Hoche. When we managed to trace him we found
he was a distant relative of the Hamburg Hoches and he invited
us to visit him in Baden Baden. He told us that although Richard
Hoche (the one who had organised the remittances) had died,
he knew where to find his widow. When we got back to
Munich, excited letters from her, as well as the other old aunts,

were awaiting us. Anna, now seventy-eight, and Lies, seventy-five, were ecstatic. Anna wrote that she had heard nothing of Edward's children since 1914, when four letters she had addressed to them in Port Pirie were returned unopened. But why had no-one thought to write to her at the end of the war, for she was still living in Bad Godesberg at her old address? (All the aunts' letters were at that time still in Jack's possession and he was still living, but it is doubtful if Frank or Puss knew they had been saved.)

This was in June of 1938. Immediate and complex arrangements were made for us to meet all the relations, who in September would come from all over Germany to one of two rendezvous. Anna and Lies both suffered so badly from asthma that neither could leave home. Timetables went back and forth, and we were begged not to let anything upset the elaborate arrangements, as Frank's three cousins, his uncle Richard's children, were taking time off work to come and meet us.

But something did upset the arrangements: Hitler's troops were massing on the frontiers of Czechoslovakia and war seemed likely. We completed our semester at Munich and, with some misgivings, spent three weeks travelling to Vienna, Budapest and Dresden, ending up in Berlin. It was mid-September. The meeting with the German relations was only days away.

At the *poste restante* in Berlin we were handed a pile of telegrams from frantic parents: 'Leave Germany at once by the shortest route, get to London and BHP will try to get you a passage on a ship home.' We left the same afternoon, crossing Holland to take an overnight ferry from Flushing to England. From London we wrote regretful letters to the devastated aunts. We were very disappointed ourselves not to be meeting them but we were on board ship in the harbour of Toulon when the Munich Pact was signed, so there could be no turning back.

On our return to Melbourne letters poured in from the aunts, who wished Frank had only let his daughters wait a few more days before ordering them home. They had known all along

Hitler would not let there be a war. 'Everyone knows and loves this rare man. Where would you find another man so ready to sacrifice himself for Volk and Vaterland? And yet so dear, and so modest.'

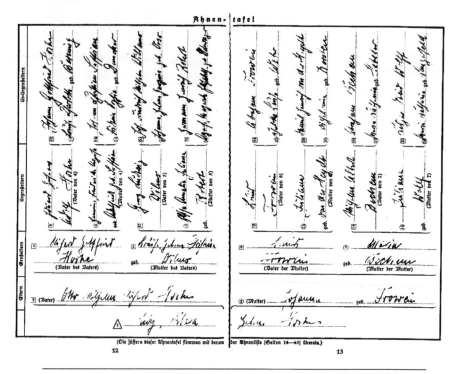

A page from a Hoche family 'ancestor pass'

It seems very unlikely that Frank's German cousins shared their aunts' views on Hitler. His only male cousin, another Richard, had the unenviable task during the Nazi era of trying to collect all the information necessary for gaining 'ancestor passes' for himself and his two sisters, obligatory if one wanted to gain, or continue in, employment. He had to provide the names and exact birth, marriage and death dates not only of the Hoches for four generations back, but of all the women and men who had married into the family. Richard sent letters to ministers of religion all over Germany, begging them to search their parish registers for him, and once, in desperation, even approached a government minister. He always wrote 'Heil Hitler' over his signature, instead of the German equivalent of 'yours sincerely', for that was the only prudent way of greeting or taking leave of people one did not know in those years. Richard must have got his information, for one of his sisters' ancestor passes has survived among the family papers.

Till war broke out in September 1939 my sister Barbara and I continued to write to the old aunts, carefully avoiding giving our opinion of Hitler. Anna reluctantly circulated our 'precious' letters among family members, claiming them back, she wrote, so as to keep them till her dying day. (Some of them she did keep as they were among her papers when they eventually came to me.) She was eager for news of all the Ferrys she used to write to, especially 'Grandmother Ferry' (who had died only six years earlier). How many of Nellie's sisters and brothers were still living? Did we know that our great-grandfather had been responsible for the whole high school sector of Hamburg?

She wrote to Frank: 'Your dear girls were like a fine meteor that fell down before having reached its aim.' He then wrote to her (surprisingly that letter has not survived), and she replied at length, though her English had suffered somewhat for lack of use.

My dear Mrs Frank and dear nephew . . . I am so rejoiced that our family has again found together and I hope so it may re-main for ever, at least as long as I am living and able to write letters . . . Your letter, dear Frank, has interested me very much . . . The last letter you sent me was in 1914, I believe. You had your occupation on Känguruh Island about opening mines, I believe, and then came nothing more . . . And we, my dear Mrs Frank, do not know each other but I hope we shall learn to know us. Your husband was that of the three Hoche children who wrote the nicest letters, long and so extended. That dear Grandy Ferry was the moving spring to this, we always thought.

She went on to tell Frank that she still had some charming greeting cards and little books which he had sent her, with illustrations and little flowers.

World War II again broke the link and it was not until April 1948 that the Hockey family again heard news of the German relatives. Anna had died in October 1944, and on going through her possessions Richard's daughter Ady had found a letter from me, written in 1938. She had been meaning to write for quite a while. She hoped I still understood enough German to be able to read the letter.

She wrote that all the Hoches had survived the bombs but most of the older generation had died from other causes. Only Edward's brother Ludwig, the doctor, and his wife, aged eighty-three and seventy-nine, were left in Hamburg and they were suffering from the great food shortage that all Germany was experiencing. Her sister Hanna, like herself a mothercraft nurse, had been barely surviving in the Russian Zone by sewing, knitting, and mending clothes for other people but had now managed to reach the British Zone. She had found work housekeeping for a family with a food-preserving factory and so was able to eat better.

The worst news was of their brother Richard (Frank's first cousin). A construction engineer in peacetime, he had been an officer in a fortifications unit in the German army, operating north of Trieste. Caught between Marshall Tito's Yugoslav Partisans and the advancing English, the unit was forced to surrender to Tito's forces on 3 May 1945. Richard was sent to a prisoner-of-war camp near Sušak on the Dalmatian coast. There he contracted typhus and was transferred to a Jugoslav military hospital in Novi-Vrbaš in Bačka, Serbia, where he died in May 1946. At the time of his death I was working in Belgrade, only a short distance away, as a member of a United Nations relief mission to Yugoslavia but, of course, neither Richard nor I knew the other was there. This was the closest the two branches of the Hoche family ever came to meeting each other.

With the death of Edward's brother Ludwig Hoche soon afterwards, the male line of Hoches had died out in Germany. I exchanged a few letters with Frank's last two cousins, Ady and Hanna, in the early post-war years, and sent them food parcels, but then we let the correspondence lapse. I was again living overseas and had a young family, and found little time for letters. Their letters lacked the spice of their Aunt Anna's, being mostly about the children of the various families where they were mothercraft nurses. I heard nothing of them until 1978, when a German woman, Ilse Lange, who had employed them in their younger days and cared for them in their old age, traced me through the Melbourne Post Office and wrote asking me what I wanted done with the Hoche papers. Both the sisters had now died and on sorting their papers she had found my address on a letter I had written to them thirty years before. I had lived at eight different addresses in three different countries in that time, but when her letter came I was living only five kilometres away from where I had lived in 1948. My husband and I visited Ilse the following year in the charming little town of Celle, in Hanover, and brought back with us the Hoche family papers and photographs and the original Hoche family tree, going back to 1603.

As I conclude my story, in 1994, it is exactly a hundred years since Eleanor Hoche died in Birdsville.

Notes on Sources

1. *South Australian Parliamentary Papers* [SAPP], 1868-9,Vol.II, No.19, Report of the Board of Education for 1867, p. 19.

2. *SAPP*, 1860,Vol. I, Report of the Board of Education for 1859, p.4.

3. Quoted in *Glimpses of Napperby Since 1840*, written by a committee to celebrate the township's centenary in 1940, out of print, p.19.

4. *SAPP*, 1860,Vol.I. Report of the Board of Education for 1859, p.4.

5. For information on registration requirements and legislation I am indebted to Dr D.H. Wilde, Registrar, Medical Board of South Australia, letter of 4 June 1990.

6. W.F. Morrison, *Aldine History of South Australia*, Vol.1, Adelaide, 1890, pp. 333–4.

7. Royal Geographical Society of Australasia (South Australian Branch) Inc., Notes for Participants in Haddon Corner Safari, September 1985

8. Theodor Hebart, *Die Vereingte Evangelisch-Lutherische Kirche in Australien: Ihr Werden Wirken und Wesen, 1838-1938,* [VELKA], Verlag Lutheran Book Depot, North Adelaide, 1938, pp. 305–65.

9. *VELKA,* p. 361.

10. C.T. Madigan, *Crossing the Dead Heart,* Rigby, Adelaide, 1946; Second Edition, 1974, p.159.

11. Madigan, p. 149.

12. John Maddock, *Mail for the Back of Beyond,* Kangaroo Press, Kenthurst, 1985, p.30.

13. Personal communication from Mr R.C. Sharman, Archivist at the Queensland Public Library in 1962, when I first started researching this story. A recent search of the police records of Birdsville in the Queensland State Archives failed to turn up this report.

14. George Farwell, *Land of Mirage,* Rigby, Adelaide, 1950; New and revised edition, Australian Pocket Books, 1960, p. 148.

15. Maddock, p. 30.

16. Sharman, pers. comm.

17. *Pugh's Almanac: The Trades, Professions and Clubs of Birdsville,* Queensland Directory, 1894, p. 49.

18. Frances Gage McGinn, *Birdsville,* pub. Wayne Cantell, 15 Boundary St, Rushcutters Bay, Sydney, 1977, no page numbers.

19. Queensland State Archives, COL/025, Letter number 05792, Divisional Board Diamantina, 1990.

20. Personal communications in 1962 from Mr F.E. Bischof, Queensland Commissioner of Police and Mr Eric Sammon, Officer in Charge, Birdsville Police.

21. Personal communication from Dr P.R. Patrick, Senior Health Officer, Queensland Department of Health, 1962.

22. Letter from Dr D.H. Wilde, 4 June 1990.

23. *Hamburg und sein Johanneum im Wandel der Jahrhunderte 1529–1929: Ein Beitrag zur Geschichte unserer Vaterstadt,* Edmund Kelter, Lütcke und Wulff, Hamburg, 1928.

24. *Hamburg und sein Johanneum,* p.184.

25. *Hamburg und sein Johanneum,* p. 173.

26. *Mittheilung des Senats an die Bürgerschaft, Erwiderung betreffend Beschwerden gegen die Amtsführung des Schulrathes Hoche,* Hamburg, 19 April 1899, Senate Document No. 76., pp. 511–40.

27. *Glimpses of Napperby,* p.19.

28. *Glimpses of Napperby,* pp. 12, 19.

29. *Glimpses of Napperby,* p.13.

30. *Glimpses of Napperby,* p.19.

31. *Glimpses of Napperby,* pp.12, 13.

32. *Glimpses of Napperby,* p.19.

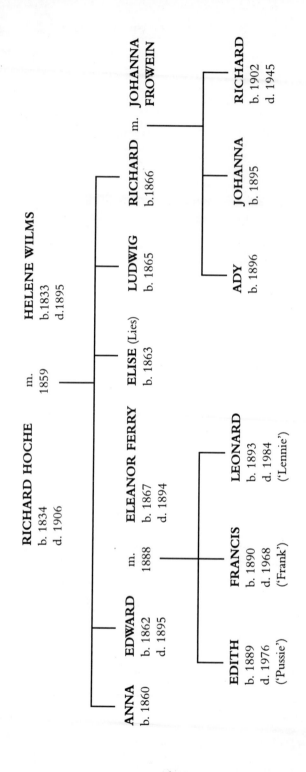

RICHARD HOCHE
b. 1834
d. 1906

HELENE WILMS
b. 1833
d. 1895

m.
1859

ANNA
b. 1860

EDWARD
b. 1862
d. 1895

m.
1888

ELEANOR FERRY
b. 1867
d. 1894

ELISE (Lies)
b. 1863

LUDWIG
b. 1865

RICHARD
b. 1866

m.

JOHANNA
FROWEIN

EDITH
b. 1889
d. 1976
('Pussie')

FRANCIS
b. 1890
d. 1968
('Frank')

LEONARD
b. 1893
d. 1984
('Lennie')

ADY
b. 1896

JOHANNA
b. 1895

RICHARD
b. 1902
d. 1945

Hoche Family

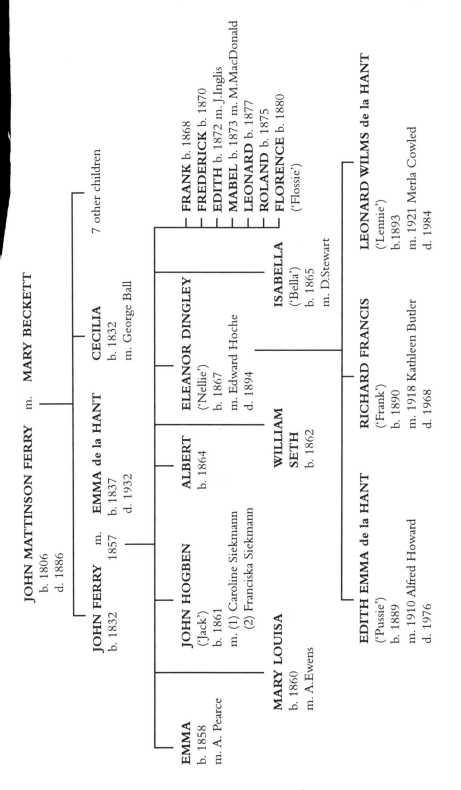

JOHN MATTINSON FERRY m. **MARY BECKETT**
b. 1806
d. 1886

7 other children

JOHN FERRY m. **EMMA de la HANT** **CECILIA**
b. 1832   1857   b. 1837   b. 1832
d. 1932   m. George Ball

EMMA **MARY LOUISA** **JOHN HOGBEN** **ALBERT** **WILLIAM SETH** **ELEANOR DINGLEY** **ISABELLA**
b. 1858 b. 1860 ('Jack') b. 1864 b. 1862 ('Nellie') ('Bella')
m. A. Pearce m. A.Ewens b. 1861 b. 1867 b. 1865
m. (1) Caroline Siekmann m. Edward Hoche m. D.Stewart
m. (2) Franciska Siekmann d. 1894

EDITH EMMA de la HANT **RICHARD FRANCIS** **LEONARD WILMS de la HANT**
('Pussie') ('Frank') ('Lennie')
b. 1889 b. 1890 b.1893
m. 1910 Alfred Howard m. 1918 Kathleen Butler m. 1921 Merla Cowled
d. 1976 d. 1968 d. 1984

FRANK b. 1868
FREDERICK b. 1870
EDITH b. 1872 m. J.Inglis
MABEL b. 1873 m. M.MacDonald
LEONARD b. 1877
ROLAND b. 1875
FLORENCE b. 1880
('Flossie')

Ferry Family

Index